"Laughing is a big deal to me! And once in a while I am fortunate to find a book that teaches me as much as it makes me laugh! That's exactly what Tim Wildmon does in his latest book, *My Life As a Half-Baked Christian*. Tim captures the reality of living a Christian life in the '90s! And he does it by putting a smile on your face. That's my kind of life-lesson."

CHONDA PIERCE,
Recording Artist, Author, and Comedienne

"Tim Wildmon takes those innermost thoughts that we all think—but usually keep to ourselves—and hangs them on the clothesline of our minds. You'll recognize them, and laugh hysterically!"

JOHNNY HART,
creator of "B.C." and "The Wizard of Id"

MY LIFE AS A HALF-BAKED CHRISTIAN

MORE TALES FROM THE FAR SIDE OF LIFE

Tim Wildmon

PROMISE PRESS
An Imprint of Barbour Publishing

© 1999 by Tim Wildmon

ISBN 1-57748-571-8

Scripture marked NIV is from the *Holy Bible: New International Version®*. NIV®. Copyright © 1973, 1978, 1984 by International Bible Society. Used by permission of Zondervan Publishing House.

Scripture marked NKJV is taken from the *New King James Version.* Copyright © 1979, 1980, 1982 by Thomas Nelson, Inc. Used by permission. All rights reserved.

Published by Promise Press, an imprint of Barbour Publishing, Inc., P.O. Box 719, Uhrichsville, Ohio 44683, http://www.barbourbooks.com

ecpa Member of the
Evangelical Christian
Publishers Association

Printed in the United States of America.

ACKNOWLEDGMENTS

To have the opportunity to write an actual manuscript, which turns into an actual book, that actual people actually buy is—actually—quite an honor. I thank the Lord for allowing this dream of having a book published become a reality.

When my first book—*I Wonder What Noah Did with the Woodpeckers*—was released I really didn't know what to expect. I didn't know if anyone would purchase it. I didn't know what people would think of my brand of sometimes-crazy humor. However, what I learned from the cards, letters, E-mails, and by visiting with people is that the vast majority of Christians enjoy a good laugh as much as anyone. Growing spiritually and enjoying ourselves are not mutually exclusive. My friend and comedian J. J. Jasper says some Christians walk around with faces so long you would think they were trying to suck golf balls out of gopher holes. It shouldn't be that way. Where did we ever get this idea that solemnness and somberness are signs of spiritual maturity?

There are several people I would like to thank for assisting me with this book. First, I want to thank my wife of fifteen years, Alison, for helping me find time to write and for being such a wonderful person. A big hug also goes to my daughter, Wriley, and my sons, Wesley and Walker. You are precious to me. Flesh of my flesh. I love you dearly.

I would also like to thank my parents, Don and Lynda Wildmon, and Alison's parents, Jim and Brenda Hardin, for being such wonderful people and the best of grandparents.

And finally, a big thank you goes to the great group of folks at Barbour Publishing/Promise Press—for making this book possible. You all have been great to work with.

INTRODUCTION

It was the best of times; it was the worst of times. The people of the land were confused, not knowing if they should be happy or sad. And so begins this happy—or sad—book, depending on how you look at it. Wait a minute, that opening has already been used by the famous writer John Grisham, I think. Okay, let's try this.

Fourscore and seven years ago our forefathers. . . our forefathers. . .did something or another but I've forgotten how the rest of that goes. Wasn't there a punch line or something? Anyway, it seems to me that I am plagiarizing again, which is not good for longevity in the world of book writing.

How about this?: Do you sleep sitting up in bed? Do people with English accents intimidate you? Is lime green your favorite color? Do you leave voice mail for yourself and end by giving your telephone number? Do you hear the voice of Barney Fife only to turn around and find no one there? If you've answered yes to any of these questions you might want to get some kind of professional help because I'm a mere humor writer and am not—I repeat, NOT—a trained psychologist, psychiatrist, or therapist of any kind. Good grief, I can't even keep up with my own eyeglasses, much less tell you where that voice is coming from. My guess is you've been watching WAY too many *Andy Griffith* reruns.

But I tell you what, if you like to have fun reading a book, you've come to the right place. I have tried writing a serious book but I just couldn't stay focused long enough to put more than one chapter together. Although the trend today seems to be toward shorter books, one-chapter books are still hard to sell. I tried using some serious run-on sentences, using dozens and dozens of words, sort of like the one you are now reading but haven't yet realized that I am running on and on and on trying to say important and significant stuff only to come up empty because I'm too busy trying to keep running this sentence on to give you an example of just how hard it is to read a twenty-five-chapter book that an author tries to jam into just one chapter but can't because he's getting tired of typing and thinking without giving it a rest. Whew! I don't know how I do it either. Some call it talent. Some call it wasted paper and trees dying in vain. I call it finger-cramping. Hey, you still there? Good. Now keep on reading.

Inside these pages I have for you some stories intended to make you laugh and have some fun, often at my own expense, of course, as you continue your Christian walk. I believe we can learn small—and sometimes large—lessons about the principles the Bible teaches from just plain old everyday living. And it's been my experience, and the experience of some of the most devoted and successful Christians I know, that if we find humor even in our failures and difficulties, it makes life a whole lot more enjoyable. As that famous philosopher Mary Poppins once sang: "A spoon full of sugar makes the medicine go down, the medicine go down, medicine go down." Why is it every time I hear that tune I just can't stop singing it over and over and over again? And I'm a thirty-six-year-old male. Maybe it's these voices in MY head? Maybe it's just that I love hearing Julie Andrews sing? Or perhaps I love singing those words because they're so true. Life sometimes clamps open our jaws and dumps bad medicine down our throats, doesn't it? Laughter, joy, and happiness are the "sugar" for me.

The title for this book (see front cover) describes many experiences I've had. Half-baked experiences. You've had them too, no doubt. I've had so many that, quite frankly, I often find myself just looking in the mirror and wondering, *Is it just you, Tim? Or do these things happen to other people? Are you a descendant of Jonah?* As I continue looking in the mirror I go deeper still and think. *And what's with the bump on the end of your nose? Is it not enough already to have a receding hairline and two chins?*

Perhaps God gives me these experiences so I can write them down and share them with readers like yourself. Perhaps God gives me these experiences to keep me humble. Or, going deep here again, perhaps God gives me these experiences to teach me lessons that will help me on down life's road. Who really knows?

Many people tell me they have Kodak Moments. Well, I'm here to tell you, I have Far Side Moments—times when I think to myself, *This is not happening to me.* Far Side Moments, I've dubbed them. If you like laughing at/with others while not having to experience the actual Far Side Moment for yourself, you'll enjoy the rest of this book. But you better get your laughs and mockery in now, my friend, 'cause ol' Brother Tim may not travel this literary road again. There is only so much finger-pointing, laughing at, and "I can't believe you actually did that," a man can take. I do have my pride. I just can't remember where I put it.

But one other note of interest you'll appreciate knowing about this author is that I recently graduated with a degree in Off-the-Wall Biblical Studies from TBW University in Saltillo, Mississippi. Yeah, my mom was impressed too. While not exactly an Ivy League school yet, it is gaining in popularity and influence with some people. People who would not give me permission to use their names. Never heard of it? Well, okay, so it's my own university. So what? The important thing is we here at TBWU (I do have sweatshirts for sale) deal with the difficult questions that other Bible scholars just won't touch and—I'm proud to say—we give you answers. I know many Americans and people from around the globe have long wanted to enrich their biblical knowledge with answers to such questions as:

- Did Adam have a navel?
- Why did David pick up five smooth stones when it only took one to kill Goliath?
- Who really started the fight, Cain or Abel?
- Why did Matthew get to go first instead of Mark, Luke, or John?
- What role did Julia Child play in the Exodus of the Israelites from Egypt?

We all want to know the answers, don't we? Be honest. After all, these are the confounding mysteries that have left thousands scratching their heads believing they had dandruff when, in fact, it was itchy questions like these swirling around in their brain and they didn't even know it. Well, ladies and gentlemen, boys and girls, plants and animals of all ages, you have come to the right place. You have purchased the right book. You have found the goose that laid the golden egg. You have turned over the rock and found the Big Fat Worm of Wisdom your mother always told you about. Yes, after every few chapters—just as a bonus that you don't have to pay extra for—I will address questions such as the above. Questions sent in from across the country. Then I will provide you with clear, concise, and definitive answers. Straight up. No beating around the bush or bushing around the beat. Again, this added value is free so you get what you paid for. And we'll even throw in a Ginzu knife for those who write and request one and can give me two good reasons why the world needs algebra. (I've talked to the Ginzu people and they tell me they have millions of these knives in a warehouse in Indiana left over from the early eighties. Said they just couldn't compete with the Time-Life and Abmaster commercials anymore.) I'm the final judge on your "two good reasons," so save your stamps. There are none.

Hey, enough with the chatter. You need to get busy reading the profound wisdom and insights found in this little book of well over one chapter and which does not plagiarize anyone. By the way, you haven't seen my eyeglasses around here anywhere, have you?

Rules of the Game

There's nothing quite like the color, pageantry, and thrill of college football for me. When I was a kid my dad would order season tickets to Mississippi State University games. I began checking the mailbox in mid-July but they would never arrive until early August. But I checked anyway. My heart leapt for joy and excitement when I finally opened the mailbox and found the manila envelope with maroon writing addressed to Don Wildmon from the Mississippi State University Athletic Department. I would hold each of the four season tickets, rolling them around in my hands with great anticipation, awaiting those Saturdays in September, October, and November when we would load up the car and drive to Jackson or Starkville to watch the Bulldogs play the likes of Auburn, LSU, Ole Miss, Florida, and Bear Bryant's Alabama teams. Those cool, crisp autumn Saturday afternoons of yesteryear serve as wonderful memories for this thirty-six-year-old little boy. I'll never forget them.

Now, twenty-five years later, Dad doesn't go to

games much anymore. He listens to them on the radio or watches them on television. At least until M-State falls three touchdowns behind. But me, I still go. Now I take my oldest son, Wesley, who is eight at the time of this writing. I began taking Wesley as a serious "student" of the game when he was six. I've actually taken him from time to time ever since he was born, but he's never really had any interest in the games despite the fact that I was training him on football long before I was training him on how to use the potty.

I had a tough time figuring that out. I just thought it was genetic or something that my son would enjoy football the way I did. But at age six it was like pulling teeth to get Wesley to go with me, and he certainly didn't share my enthusiasm for the games.

Usually he asked a few minutes into the game when we were going home. Now, I certainly attribute some of this to the fact that he may well have been burned out—given the fact that he attended his first college football game when he wasn't quite five months old. State lost to archrival Ole Miss in Jackson that afternoon. I was so upset I accidentally left the lil' fellow at the stadium and got twenty miles up I-55 before I realized what I had done. When I returned to the stadium he was still there and was as upset as I. And he was a little chilly. But other than that he was okay. I felt really bad about it and, needless to say, Alison was not a happy camper and let me know in no uncertain terms I was letting college football have far too much control over my emotions and what bit of frazzled brain I had left.

"What do you know about football anyway?" I said in a 4-3 defensive response. "You're a girl."

This was a bad choice of words. It was on that day I learned what a quarterback feels like when he gets blindsided. I never even saw it coming, folks. She took me out of the game with one play. A girl.

Well, I talked Wesley into going to the first game of the season on September 2, 1995, in Starkville against Memphis State University. Just Wesley and me. Fortunately, when we arrived at the stadium the pre-game festivities including the band show and the parachutist landing with the game ball at midfield were enough to hold his attention. *This is great,* I thought, *Wesley is finally starting to enjoy coming with me.* Then sure enough, after about a quarter he began the "when are we going home" drill.

Not again, I thought to myself. *This is football, son; this is America! Don't whine to me. Fried chicken, ice tea, the Statue of Liberty, Elvis, and football—this is who we are. You don't want to grow up a social retard do you, Wes? No, you most certainly don't. Now start paying attention here.* It was all I could do not to verbalize what I was thinking. But I couldn't force my love for a game on my little son, no matter how much I wanted to at the moment.

"It will be over in a lil' while, Wesley. Do you want a coke?" I asked, trying to change the subject and hopefully buying myself fifteen more minutes before he would ask me again about leaving. (For future reference, in the South, the word "coke" is a generic term for all soft drinks. The Coca-Cola Company—based out of Atlanta, Georgia, loves this.)

But after a couple of delay-tactic answers again—and it's hard to keep coming up with these when you're passionately into a college football game—something new came to my ever-expanding and sometimes-contracting mind. A profound thought it was. *You know Tim,* I thought to myself, *Wesley doesn't understand what's going on down there on the field. All he sees is a bunch of people in uniforms running wildly around on a painted field with a funny shaped ball, hitting each other, and stopping occasionally to separate because some guys dressed like zebras run around blowing whistles and waving their arms. And as for the people in the stands, including his dad, they make loud noises, clap their hands, and yell things at the people on the field who can't hear a word they're saying because everyone is trying to talk—or yell—at once. That's football through Wesley's eyes,* I thought. I would want to know when we were going home too if I was Wesley. In the words of Ricky Ricardo, I needed to do a little "splainin" to Wesley.

"Do you know what's going on out there, Wesley?"

He shook his head "no" as he sipped on a watered-down coke, which—like cold hot dogs—are a staple at college football games.

"Let me tell you," I began explaining to Wesley.

"You see the Bulldogs in maroon and you see the Tigers in blue, well. . ."

I took about ten minutes and explained in terms as simple as possible (which is not hard for me) the object of the game and the meaning and purpose for the actions. I pointed out the scoreboard, the clock, and how to score points. I taught him as the action went along. He didn't grasp everything, by any means, but he did begin to watch the action and ask me questions. He was now somewhat interested in the game. He didn't ask again when we were going home.

A lot of times we look at life the way Wesley was viewing the football game that September evening. It all looks chaotic and it's difficult to make any sense of it. The Bible—our playbook for life—says a lot about wisdom and understanding. We gain knowledge, wisdom, and understanding through prayer, listening, reading the Scriptures, and experience. We will never fully grasp everything about life or living, nor, quite frankly, do I think we want to. Only God knows all. However, He does give us direction and guidance for everyday living when we seek Him. The key is seeking the Lord on a consistent basis. My experience has been that those who are following Christ are able to understand and cope with life much better than those who are lost or without the light of Christ.

Well, now, back to the game and I'll answer the question I know you're dying to know the answer to: Who won? Yes, Mississippi State was victorious. But then—that's right—they lost the next game. Afterward I had to explain to Wesley why the Bulldogs don't win every game. He told me we needed a quarterback change, while I opined we needed better play calling by the head coach. If only the coach would listen to us fans in the stands he wouldn't lose any games and save us all a lot of grief!

Hey, what can I say? Everybody loves a winner. We're Americans.

Two Things to Remember

1. "If any of you lacks wisdom, let him ask of God, who gives to all liberally and without reproach, and it will be given to him" (JAMES 1:5 NKJV).
2. If you don't like college football, you should leave this country immediately. You are not a good American.

Pizza Party

One of the reasons God gives us children is to test our patience and will. This I believe. And the place where kids do this most often is in public. Church, grocery stores, ball games, and restaurants are favorite places of youngsters for testing parents. And if there is one thing I am an expert on, it's kids and restaurants. I've given serious thought to writing a book on the subject. You see, Alison and I are big-time supporters of the Tupelo Restaurant Association. We see it as a civic duty. And we hold firm to the belief that if we use our kitchen too much it will devalue our home. Granted, this is an unconventional way of looking at property value, but a logical one, I think you would agree.

Yes, one of the weaknesses Alison and I have is that we like to eat out. I guess it's a weakness; that's the way our parents kind of look at it anyway. But there's a reason for this. There's a line in the "Song of the South" that says, "Somebody told us Wall Street fell, but we were so poor we couldn't tell." That verse describes many folks who lived back in the 1930s and '40s.

Our parents were raised in rural Mississippi back in those days. This was back when most everyone had a garden, a cellar (later replaced by the refrigerator), and chickens running around in the front yard. Especially out in the country. The chicken, which means "rotisserie" in French, was served only on special occasions. . .like when the preacher came over for Sunday lunch.

When it came time for one of the chickens to go inside the house—wink, wink—someone had to go out and "wring the little chicken's neck," then defeather the bird by hand. Pluck is the correct word, I think. Then you had to boil the bird to make sure all the feathers were off. Feathers ruin the taste. That's about as much as I know.

Now what I'm telling you here is just what I picked up from my parents, Alison's parents, and a lot of talks with my grandparents. I assume this is where the phrase, "I'm going to wring your neck!" comes from, that some parents still use when they get angry with their kids—not that I ever threaten mine with such violence, you understand. But I have heard other parents utter such things, especially in restaurants.

The upside of eating out, of course, is that you don't have to prepare, cook, or clean up after a family of three small children makes an awful mess all over the table, floor, and surrounding area. The downside, however, is you have to decide what to order with the children all talking at once, and at some places you have to leave a tip. Which leads me to:

CHILDREN AND FOOD ESTABLISHMENTS
by Tim Wildmon

I have three children. Wriley is nine at the time of this writing, and she's my daughter. Wesley, age seven, and Walker, age three, are my boys. Recently we were in a Mexican restaurant we like to frequent in Tupelo. Best salsa dip north of the border. Alison and I prefer Mexican or Italian when we're feeling international. Most places we can split a fajita. Except when we forget where we are and order one in Vanelli's—the Italian place we like—also in Tupelo. Here's a little tip we learned that may help some of you avoid some needless embarrassment. Move in a little closer and I'll whisper it: They don't serve fajitas at Italian restaurants. Yeah, I was a little surprised also. But, it's true.

Every once in a while Alison and I will order a chicken-steak combo, but most of the time we want just steak as our fajita meat. Why I tell you this, I don't know. I just thought you might be wondering. Maybe in a real detailed psychological profile, this would say something about our personalities. Or maybe we just like the taste of red meat better and—subconsciously— we think about chickens running around with their heads cut off and it has a negative effect on our taste buds. Although, I suppose, if we were to dwell on what happens to cattle at the slaughterhouse, we would not be too keen on beef either. Whatever the reasons, we almost always order steak fajita.

The kids usually order something small and we give them some food off our plate. I guess that's redneck behavior, but hey, we're southern born and southern bred and that's just the way we were raised. "Don't waste food," was drilled into our heads while growing up. "Chinese children are starvin'," our parents said. "So why are they sending us all this rice?" I asked Mom on several occasions, pointing out the little Oriental person on the rice package. Sometimes Mom got frustrated with this question.

Anyway, Alison asked Wesley if he wanted some of the meat from our fajita. As all parents know, kids are each different when it comes to the food they do or don't like. And they'll tell you so. Sometimes, they have very strange ways that they like their food prepared. I've given up trying to figure this out. My philosophy now is: *If you want to eat your hamburger upside down with only one pickle hanging out of the left side of the bun or with tartar sauce and a granola bar sandwiched in between two french fries, go ahead. Whatever floats your boat. Just eat the hamburger.*

Wesley, he likes the meat just a certain way and doesn't care for the tortilla. So Alison generously gave him some of our meat—my meat—and placed it on his plate. We are good parents. "If you run out of plate, you can always use the table," is my way of looking at it. But that's kind of redneckish also, and some people stare. But I figure if you're "payin' for the table," you might as well get your money's worth, right?

Wesley began chewing *some* of the beef. I looked over at him as he moved the meat around in his mouth for about ten seconds and then he said, "This meat tastes funny; it's burned or sumpin'."

To which I responded, "Well then, put it back."

Of course, I meant the portion of meat he *still had on his plate* which had heretofore gone unchewed. Any eight-year-old with half a brain would have known what I meant. Wesley, in perfect seven-year-old reasoning, looked at me wide-eyed in, "Okay, if you say so," fashion, raised his hand to his open mouth and was fully prepared to give the fajita cud back to his mother and I. You read that right. I stopped him just short of flinging the meat back onto our hot plate amid the onions and bell peppers. Lucky us, because it would have been indistinguishable in there and could have very well ruined his parents' meal. You've seen fajita plates; you know what I mean. Most of the meat looks pre-chewed already and besides, who really knows for sure? We are—after all—talking about a restaurant that serves refried beans, remember.

"No, no! Not the meat in your mouth! The meat on the plate you haven't touched! What's wrong with you, boy?" I said in disgust. (When writing this my loving wife, Alison, said the term "boy" was pejorative and that I should have used "son" instead. I told her Wesley needed a little pejorative—which means "jacking up" in Greek—when he does things like this. "Besides," I said, "since when did you start using the word 'pejorative' anyway?")

To put it mildly, I was exasperated—which is something I don't get very often, seeing that I have a hard time pronouncing it—with my eldest male offspring.

By this time Walker has knocked over his drink and I noticed some foreign substance on my tie. I decided no one would care, since we were in a foreign restaurant after all.

HERE WE MOVE TWO WEEKS HENCE.

Time: 6:47 P.M.

Place: An Italian restaurant somewhere in Tupelo, Mississippi. The establishment was already mentioned in this story for those who were paying attention, but will go unnamed here to protect their business—as some people would no longer consider patronizing it if they thought the Wildmons might happen to be there at the same time.

As is our custom, Alison and I asked for a booth as far away as possible from other people who might just be there to enjoy their dinner. Imagine that? Some people want the world. Smoking, nonsmoking, nuclear waste section—it doesn't matter as long as we're safely removed from the PWWUC (People-Who-Wouldn't-Understand Crowd), otherwise known as

People Who Don't Have Three Children Under Ten. Sometimes we get our wish, other times not.

On this particular evening, we pointed out the booth we wanted and were promptly seated. This is another thing I consider in a restaurant: How fast can we be seated? If you wait around too long, the kids— especially three-year-olds—seem to roam farther and farther from your bench. If we have to wait more than fifteen minutes, we miss our call because we have to get them out of the street, kitchen, or bathroom where they are talking to total strangers under the stalls. On this evening the hostess, the person who hands you the menu or whatever they're called, quickly rattled off the something–something special (which we never hear because they don't wait long enough for a family with three children under ten to get situated) and went back to her post. She could say, "Our soup of the day is pig slop," and we'd never know it. We'd just say thanks and begin looking at the menu.

"Honey, did she say pig slop?"

"I don't know; what's in it? Where is it on here?"

"Walker, would you get your foot off my groin area, son?"

If you have children, you understand.

We were in a good six-seat booth with plenty of padding to muffle the eating/talking/yelling/fighting/correcting/silverware-clanging noises that sometimes come from our table. The table just across the aisle— about four feet—was unoccupied for the first ten minutes of this experience. Alison and I like this kind of privacy. Then, as we made our way through the lasagna and spaghetti buffet with our kids, a man in his forties and his young daughter of about twelve, were seated at this table just across from our little family. Being at the buffet, I had to balance my half-full plate to rush over—just out of curiosity—and see if I couldn't hear what the person who seats people said about the soup of the day. But I missed it again and almost served the fellow lasagna without him ever having to go through the buffet line. And I lost my place in line, even though I told Wesley to hold it for me. The ten or so people behind us got kind of irritated at this and pushed their way on past lil' Wes. He tried for his daddy, though. Physically held 'em off for two or three minutes. I told him I was proud of the effort.

Anyway, the man sitting across from us looked clean, neat, and was dressed in a pressed pair of slacks and a button-down shirt. Nice-looking guy. Had a short beard that was neatly trimmed around the edges. Something I can never quite do. His daughter was sitting up straight and had a dress on, and tidy, pretty long hair. Probably an only child. They sat across from one another and talked quietly. These were the kind of people who don't mix their food, eat one dish at a time, and cut the lettuce up in their salad whether it needs it or not. *Re*fined folks for northeast Mississippi.

Meanwhile, four feet over was The Wildmon Family Here to Brighten Your Day. I didn't like the looks or the feel of this situation we—by the way—had not asked for.

We were doing fairly well there for a while and I was proud of the gang for those two or three minutes. Then I had to go and bring up *the* subject. Stupid, really. Although at the time I didn't think too much about it and was just making what I thought was light conversation when I said softly, "Now when we get home tonight, everyone's got to get a bath."

This is not an unusual request made by parents.

WHOA! I had forgotten. These were the Christmas holidays and the kids didn't have to go to school for two more weeks. So Wriley—ironically the cleanest and most hygiene-conscious member of the threesome by far—reacts rather loudly and abruptly, "But Dad, you said we didn't have to get a bath till Christmas Eve!"

Yes, the man and young girl heard it. Clearly. They couldn't help but hear. Half the restaurant heard it.

We were three days out from Christmas Eve and I did give the kids a day off from their nightly baths during holidays, but Wriley was badly mistaken. Obviously she had miscounted and misunderstood what I had said. I looked straight at Alison. Speechless. I sat in stunned silence, suspended in time and space, with my spaghetti-stringing fork at about eye level. It was surreal, really. I then said to Alison through my teeth, as the man and young girl turned and looked at our table (I could see this out of my peripheral vision—I didn't dare stare back), "Must we. . .must we talk about our family bathing habits here? Now?"

Alison began to turn red and burst out in laughter as only she can. All this is happening while our three-year-old son Walker mentioned quietly—at least twice—he had to take care of business in the little boys' room. We heard him, but you can understand why we didn't respond immediately. Now sensing what to him seemed like a good time for all, and wanting to make his mother laugh even harder, he decided to yell out, "I GOTTA GO POTTY!" Twice he did this while laughing out loud.

This is not happening, I thought, still suspended in time and space along with my spaghetti strings, some of which were giving way to gravity. *I can take a lot Lord, You know I can. I'm not easily embarrassed, but why this? Why do we have to ruin this man's father-daughter night out that they've probably been planning for months? People know me here, Lord. I'm a deacon in my church. This man is probably going to go to the phone right now and report me to my Promise Keepers small group or something. God, do You even care?*

This is all still happening in slow motion. I can feel the weight of the stares from those around us. Like one of those old E.F. Hutton commercials, it was as if the place became silent and everyone had stopped what they were doing. The cooks came out of the kitchen, the other customers stopped eating, and someone had turned a spotlight on our booth now that Walker had taken it upon himself to share his physical feelings with everyone within a two-block area.

After a couple of minutes we regained some sense of composure and I took Walker on to the men's room where the "potty" is located. I entertained the idea of staying in there or going on to the car as I didn't relish the thought of walking right in front of the man and his daughter again after what had just taken place at our table.

But we washed our hands and headed back. *Please let them be gone,* I thought. Nope. Still there. *Well, I might as well make the best of it.*

"Hi, how y'all doin'?" I said with a smile as the gentleman looked up at me. He didn't smile and didn't speak. I thought to myself, as I grew really defensive: *What are you staring at? Hey, buddy, you oughta try this. I got a mind to reach over there and sling a little spaghetti sauce on that white button-down of yours and see how ya like that there, Mister Got-it-all-together. How 'bout some Thousand Island in that beard and some pasta on those pretty pants? Yeah, howdja like that! Huh! Show you how the other half lives!*

Tim, calm down.

Okay, I am calm.

Well, I've been around this family thing for a long time now. I've been in a managerial position since Wriley Hope was born in 1987. Sometimes I don't want to manage anymore. Especially when the children disobey, fuss, talk back, or do something else that takes the joy out of parenting. The couple of experiences I've shared here are fairly innocent and trivial. (My friends in their forties laugh and tell me to just wait, it gets "better" with the teenage years.) But kids can do a lot of different things—and some can get real creative—to test their parents' patience and will to be, well, parents. God has ordained authority over children. We should be willing to bend some; I think good parents learn when to push an issue and when to allow kids an opportunity to see the error of their ways on their own. But the bottom line is, it is the responsibility of parents to teach children right from wrong, good behavior from bad behavior—in public as well as in private.

Now would you pardon me for a moment? I've got to go the restroom and get a wet towel. While correcting my kids I dropped a perfectly good piece of pizza in my lap.

Two Things to Remember

1. Generally speaking, children are a reflection of the time, energy, and effort parents put into teaching and training them.
2. In case you missed it, Walker said he's GOTTA GO POTTY!

LIFE'S GRIND

"Mountain, be thou removed.

"Mountain, be thou removed.

"Mountain, be THOU removed."

I barely opened one eye. The mountain was still there. I continued.

"Okay. Last chance, mountain. Be thou removed. . . please."

The mountain called my bluff.

"*What* are you doing?" Alison said as she walked into our bedroom.

"Well, baby, I've had it with ironing. I was hoping that if I prayed hard enough the Lord would take this mountain of clothing from me," I responded.

As a man of the nineties, ironing, like life's daily grind, is always before me. Life is hard sometimes. And I realize I have it easy compared to a lot of folks. Single parents come to mind, for example. But back to my asking the Lord to take the ironing from me.

"You ever heard the phrase 'taking the Bible out of context,' Tim?"

"Well, yeah, but let me ask you a question 'in context.' Who came up with this idea of ironing anyway? What makes pressed shirts any better than wrinkled shirts? Think about it. Wrinkled is a shirt's natural state, no? It appears to me someone with nothing better to do came along and invented what we now call an iron and duped millions of people into thinking they have to have one."

"Well, you're entitled to your wild speculations, I suppose, but you're going to burn a hole in your shirt if you don't quit talkin' and get that iron off," Alison said as she nodded her head toward the ironing board and folded a towel.

I quickly turned back around and pulled the iron off, barely saving one of my better shirts.

"See there, see that. If I wasn't doing this, that never would have happened. It's a Chinese plot, I tell you. I've got a new novel title for Tom Clancy; it's called *Red Iron Burning*. It'll be about how the Chinese are just waiting for the day all American men are ironing and BOOM, they'll take football off the air and replace it with Ping-Pong. It's going to happen, Al, you just watch. It's prophecy."

"You know, maybe you should take a break," Alison said, stopping her folding for a minute. "This is really getting to you."

Yes, ladies and gentlemen, for the most part, I do the ironing in this family. Now I know what you're thinking. You're thinking, *What a waste of intellectual dynamite that, if harnessed, and not wasted on time spent ironing, could change the face of the world as we know it and lead to peace, understanding, and goodwill among peoples of all races, creeds, and nationalities.* Well, I'm thinking somewhat the same thing, but more along the lines of watching a little more basketball *in addition to* fostering peace, understanding, and goodwill among peoples of all races, creeds, and nationalities.

Seeing that I iron almost every night, I have a few fine points of pressing etiquette I like to follow. One is *I like to always have the iron turned on when I use it.* This is very important. You've done it—started pressing only to discover there's no heat, no steam, to get the wrinkles out. Again, the first step to a successful pressing experience: Turn iron on.

Second, I like steam to come out of my Sunbeam 2000 (I added the 2000 because it just sounds more masculine) and I want it accompanied by the customary noise an iron makes when it gives off steam. *Shhhhhhahah* is basically how it sounds. I love that sound. I often say this back to my iron: "Shhhhhhhahah the man!" I say in response. In human relationships, this is called bonding. I'm basically saying to my little household appliance friend, "You and me, bud. I'll push, you keep steaming, I'll give you water and let you up for air every few minutes and yes, indeed, we'll conquer this mass of cotton and nylon, together, by midnight." And my iron calls back to me, "Shhhhhhhahah, master! We shall indeed overcome."

Although generally thought of as an inanimate object, for me at least, it's important that I see my iron as a partner in this labor camp I call home, much like an old farmer may have bonded with his mule. We sweat together. We take on pleats with a passion not unlike a farmer and mule taking on hardened soil. (Alison has adopted a "don't ask, don't tell" policy with me on this "relationship." As long as I get the ironing done, she cares not about what motivational techniques I utilize to accomplish the task. I admire her for not feeling threatened.)

I am constantly making sure the water level is where I can see it. I can't stand to dry iron. Don't ask me why; it's just one of my little quirks. The other night my water level was getting dangerously low which—for me—means I can't see water in the little clear window. If you can't see the water, you're getting way too close to dry ironing for my comfort zone. It's like driving a car long after your gas gauge has been below the red area. So I went to the bathroom to get a cup of water and discovered a glass already filled with water. I assumed someone had gotten a drink and had just left what remained in the cup. So, I—ever the conservationist—took it over to the iron and poured it all in and continued to iron. This was a big mistake, I would quickly learn. It wasn't but a couple of minutes and my trusty little Sunbeam began making terrible, strange noises and spitting the water back out its spout. It was the weirdest ironing experience I've ever had, and I, my friends, am an ironing veteran of many years. I have been around the ironing block a few times. I've seen a lot, but nothing to prepare me for this.

"Alison, come back here and look at this baby," I yelled up front and then stood back in amazement. For some reason, my little household appliance friend was turning on me. It was in utter rebellion, just spraying and sputtering. It was bucking on the board. It turned ugly. Occasionally, little brown dots of water would come forth in volcanic fashion. Then, to make things worse, it began emitting an awful odor. It smelled strangely like burnt sugar.

"What in the world have you done to my iron?" Alison said as she entered the room, looked at me, and then back at the iron. I stepped back farther from the machine to watch this twilight-zone spectacle.

"I ain't done nothin'," I said in good around-the-house Southern English. "I just got the cup of water from the bathroom and poured it in the iron and it started having a fit."

"You didn't get the cup beside the sink, did you?"

"Well, yeah. It was full of water. What's the deal?"

"No, no, baby. That's the cup of clear Gatorade I brought back here for Walker this afternoon."

"Oh."

"I just bought that iron. Couldn't you tell it wasn't water?"

This, readers, is what's known as a rhetorical question. Rhetorical questions are usually asked in frustration or to make the one being questioned admit he is an idiot.

Now, to me, ironing is a metaphor for life. And we all have our own private metaphors for life, don't we? For some it's farming. For others, flying kites. Still others, where I live, see frog gigging as a metaphor for life. Whatever yours is, I'm not here to judge it. I simply ask that you respect mine: ironing. How so, you ask? Well, God has blessed me with a wonderful life. I have a beautiful wife, three healthy children, and a good job. And so many other blessings. So I'm not complaining. But still, like that perpetual pile of clothing in the basket that greets me each evening, the everyday routine of life—the daily grind, I call it—is always there. And this grind, well, it can wear me down sometimes. My body gets tired. My mind gets tired. My soul gets tired. It catches up with all of us from time to time, doesn't it? Raising children, doing an honest day's work at the office, church activities, domestic chores, paying bills, et cetera, takes a toll on the average American adult. And it's easy to get these priorities out of order. (That is, of course, if we can find time to get them out of order.)

It is both unreasonable and unrealistic to expect God to make life easy for us. The Bible promises no such escape. But the Lord does promise His children that He is with them all the time—through life's daily grind. He is the source of our mental, physical, emotional, and—most certainly—our spiritual strength. We can lean on our Heavenly Father for our rest and our restoration when we tire or are caught up in the stress and pressures of today's world.

Jesus put it this way in Matthew 11:28–30 (NIV): "Come to me, all you who are weary and burdened, and I will give you rest. Take my yoke upon you and learn from me, for I am gentle and humble in heart, and you will find rest for your souls. For my yoke is easy and my burden is light."

As for my iron, it still stinks. As does ironing, for that matter. All I can say is, "Shhhhhhhhhahah! I will press on."

Two Things to Remember

1. God tells us we can lean on Him to find strength for the ups and downs of daily living.
2. One great thing about being Americans is that we can have our favorite metaphor and yet respect the opinion of our neighbor who may have a different favorite metaphor.

THE FAMILY WAY

One recent July evening, my brother-in-law Neal called and invited our family to go skiing the following weekend. I would have invited Neal and my sister Donna first, but I didn't have a boat. Still don't. And if you're going to go water-skiing, a boat is essential. I went without a boat one time. Trust me, it's no fun swimming all the way out to the middle of the lake with your skis on and basically treading water for three hours while attempting to flag down a boat. It was that day I realized that America had changed. People are cold and unsympathetic nowadays. They just don't pick up hitch-hiking skiers like they used to. There was a day, not too long ago, when people didn't lock their houses, when dope meant a dumb person, and when a man could swim out in almost any lake or river in America—with just his skis and life jacket—and it wouldn't be any time before a friendly soul would gladly stop and throw him a rope. Not anymore. Do that today and people just ignore you or laugh and pass on by. Some teenagers, if they know you're boatless, play this little game where they see how close they can get to the "ski bum" without actually hitting you. It's a different world out there on the waterways of America, folks. A different world altogether.

"Sure," Alison told Neal over the phone. "We would love to go."

When Alison and I married in 1984, we vowed our children were going to have as happy a childhood experience as possible. Life is short and the time parents have with their children at home is even shorter. Ours had been youthful years filled with fond memories. We wanted the same for our own kids. One day Wriley, Wesley, or Walker may find fault with their mama and daddy, but it won't be because we didn't spend time with them.

So we met Neal, Donna, and my sister Angela at Bay Springs, which is a recreational area on the Tennessee-Tombigbee Waterway up the Natchez Trace Parkway about forty miles north of Tupelo. It's also just five minutes from the now-abandoned country farm where my grandparents raised four children (my mom, her sister, and two brothers) in the hills of Tishomingo County.

We brought our two sons, Wesley, eight, and Walker, three, who along with Donna and Neal's boys—Neal Russell, four, and Drew, two—rounded out the Cotton-top Four-some. I should say the Cotton-top Fearless Foursome because this quartet of blond-headed Southern boys were not the least bit scared of the water, despite their age. Well, you wouldn't expect Wesley to be, but neither were Walker and Neal, the reason obviously being that they were fresh off their first "tadpole" swimming lessons which—in their minds—made them fit to swim the English Channel. Every chance they got, the boys jumped out of the boat into the water, did their little half swim/half dog paddle, and whooped and hollered. Southern boys learn early the fine art of whoopin' and hollerin'.

The summer's day went by, my heart better for having seen my sons and nephews laughing and having a ball. I tucked away a lifelong memory that afternoon.

What is it about children laughing that makes us grown-ups feel so good? Maybe we remember the fun we had as children. For me it's therapeutic. It washes my soul. *But oh for the days,* I thought. The childhood days of few responsibilities where high stress was having the chain come off my bike. . .

By the time we pulled the boat out of the water the sun had set behind the pine trees, putting to bed one scorcher of a day. But we had "suffered" through it. We loaded our boys in the van and I remarked to Alison that it been nearly three years since we moved my granddad and grandmother Bennett from their little country farmhouse to Traceway Manor in Tupelo, and I hadn't been back there since. This was due to my granddad's failing health. He died just a few months after the move.

"I'd like to drive by and take a look at the old place

for a minute while we're so close," I said.

Alison agreed and we drove down the winding road for a few minutes—the only sign of life being an occasional front porch light from one of the few homes along the way—until we made it to my grandparents' house. I turned into the front yard which was covered, almost like giant mushrooms, by two huge oak trees. Grass and weeds had now taken over this once well-worn area. *This isn't right*, I thought. *Grandmother's station wagon and Granddad's pickup should be parked here.* I shone my bright lights ahead to what remained of a small house that had burned down a year or so after we moved my grandparents out.

"Turn on your brights," Alison said.

"They're on," I responded. It was pitch-black.

"I want to see if the barn is still standing," I said to Alison as I got out of the van by myself and walked closer. The barn was just a couple of hundred feet from the back of the house and I couldn't make it out. It was that dark and I couldn't see to walk back. I later learned that it had been torn down. My mind began to wander back to my boyhood years.

This yard was where my granddad first put me on a Shetland pony he bought just for his grandkids when I was one year old—1964. Those steps led to the front porch, which was screened to keep the bugs and dogs out. There were always three or four dogs hanging around the yard, waiting for my grandmother to bring out the leftover scraps after supper.

I spent a lot of summer nights in a swing on that porch—the only sounds being the crickets and the humming of the window air-conditioning unit that dripped water into an old coffee can. You could hear a car coming from two miles away. Lightnin' bugs played here and there.

The first and only time I ever plowed a field with a mule was on that farm. Granddaddy used a John Deere tractor for the big fields, but still kept a mule around for his garden until the early seventies. He let me have the reigns when I was eight. The mule started going and I couldn't get him to stop—despite my pleas of "Whoa! You dumb mule!" The beast dragged me thirty yards, plowing with my feet all the way, before Granddad came over and took control. Scared me to death. I was shook. But he laughed. Oh, how Granddad laughed.

This was also the place where I learned to "slop the pigs." I loved jumping over the fence into the pigpen for this task that most detested. Yeah, it was muddy and smelly. But I liked it that way.

Then I recalled the many, many Christmases spent in this burned-out home with my aunts, uncles, and cousins. Thirty-one consecutive for me. When we were little kids, Granddad would gather us around and "count our ribs" until we collapsed in tears of laughter.

"Count mine, Granddad," we would all say. He would play with us until he tired out. We "lil' uns"—as he affectionately called us—could have gone on all night.

I walked back to the van, stepped out of the summer night's thick air and back inside the comfort of our cool van. I thought about how life changes. Good times. Bad times. They come and go. Sad thing is, I can never go back again. I suppose it's sad, especially when I get in such a melancholy mood. I often tell my three-year-old Walker I'm going to give him "stay little" pills so he won't grow up on me.

God is the giver of life. Time is such a precious gift. What better way to spend that gift than with our family? Loving them, making them happy, maybe giving them a little slice of heaven right here on Earth.

Two Things to Remember

1. We need to thank the Lord every day for family and friends who make our lives richer.
2. Mules do what they wish with eight-year-old boys and care not if you insult their intelligence by using adjectives such as "dumb" when yelling at them.

HALF-BAKED

The story you are about to read is true. The names have not been changed because basically they are my family and if they didn't want to end up in a story of mine, then they shouldn't be hanging around me. I tell you this ahead of time, that the following account is the absolute truth, because I know you're not going to believe me. But I have my "honest-as-the-day-is-long" baby brother, Mark Ellis Wildmon, to back me up on it, so if you don't trust me, you can ask him.

A couple of summers back, Mark, my brother-in-law Neal Clement, my dad, and I went canoeing on the Buffalo River up around Savannah, Tennessee. Men have to do these things every once in a while to bond and get back to nature. We have an innate desire—we men—to prove to ourselves that we can survive in the wilderness on pork-and-beans, wild game, and fish if we have to. Either that, or we grew up watching Fess Parker play Daniel Boone on television in the late sixties—early seventies—and we want to be kids again.

During my childhood my backyard served as my

own personal Kentucky backwoods. Just like Dan'l Boone. If I really wanted to venture off into parts unknown where wild beasts (such as rabbits) and savages (such as fourteen-year-old Tony Anderson) roamed, I would go out into the field behind our house which backed up to the Big Star grocery store. The field was ripe with all kinds of berries that made for tasty afternoon snacks when eight-year-old boys got tired of chasing imaginary bears. But when you reach "mature" adulthood and have the itch to play wilderness hero, you can't very well tell your wife and children you're going to "play Daniel Boone" in the backyard. Instead, we go off to the woods where adult men can pretend and role-play safe from ridicule.

However, I did try this once in my own backyard when I was twenty-eight. But Alison threatened to leave me when our pastor dropped by—unannounced as they always do, I might add—to talk to us about teaching a young-marrieds' Sunday school class, only to find me in our pup tent with my muzzle loader and coonskin hat on. He got kind of startled when he approached and I yelled out from inside the tent, "Stop right there, you ugly bear or your hide is mine!" Well, I didn't know who it was and I was in character. But it really embarrassed Alison and she made me quit my little escape-from-reality games.

Anyhow, Mark and I were in one canoe, Dad and Neal in the other. I had suggested we pull a third canoe in tow just in case one of ours sank—just to be on the safe side—but Mark, Dad, and Neal thought it would be cumbersome and make it more difficult to maneuver.

"Are you a loon?" were Mark's exact words. Dad and Neal looked at each other in obvious agreement with Mark's sentiments. I thought about it a minute and agreed. Four heads are better than one sometimes, even when that one head is Tim Wildmon's, amazing as that may seem.

Midway through the second day we came to this nice, easy, slow-flowing spot in the river—a great place to fish—so Mark and I picked up our rods and went to it. We were bass fishing with spinner bait but having little luck. I think it was the way the moon was shaped the night before or the fact that the water was too high or too low that particular day; I'm not sure which. I just know it couldn't have been our angling abilities because—not to boast—they are ample. Like all good Southern fishermen, we do watch Bill Dance each week and know full well how to catch largemouth bass. But let's just say, on this particular trip, it was a good thing we brought plenty of Vienna sausage and crackers. However, at this stop, after about twenty minutes or so of casting and reeling, Mark got a strike.

"Reel Big Deddy in, bro!" I said to Mark.

"He doesn't feel like Big Deddy, Tim," Mark responded quietly.

"Compared to what we've caught so far today, Mark, you've got Big Deddy on the line there, potna."

Mark reeled "Big Deddy" in after ten seconds of

brutal man-to-fish combat, his rod's tip barely bent. The largemouth was one pound if he was anything. It was a special moment for Mark and me. I was proud to be his brother.

"I almost feel like we're one, Mark."

"What are you talkin' about?" he said bewildered, looking out at the water as he reeled and spit.

"You know. It's been a while since we've been out in the wild together like this depending on each other like we are. You paddle, I steer. You whistle, I tap. You catch and clean, I eat. We're one here, Mark."

"Wrong, buddee! I catch, I eat. You starve."

Now what happened next was the unbelievable part. A freak of nature the likes of which I hadn't seen before and haven't seen since. And I know freaks of nature when I see them. I'm a longtime veteran patron of the Mississippi-Alabama Fair & Livestock Show where as a kid I saw with my own eyes the bearded lady, the two-headed calf, and the pig with six legs. If I'm lying I'm dying.

Mark took the monster off the hook and began to filet the fish in short order. Under normal conditions— i.e., we catch a lot of big fish—Mark would have thrown this fellow back in. But not this day. He was our happy meal. Using a sharp knife, Mark quickly cleaned one side of the bass down to the bone and turned it over to finish the task. (Fish have two sides— for you ladies.) However, in the process, Mark accidentally let Big Deddy slip out of his hand and back into the river. We both looked down in the clear water, Mark attempting to save our next meal with his bare hands when suddenly he stopped, stunned at what he was witnessing. The bass—one side skeleton—was swimming alongside our canoe like he didn't want to leave. You read that right; the fish slowly (for obvious reasons) swam beside us. Of course, due to his physically challenged state, the poor lil' fella was swimming in circles, which may have had something to do with the fact that he wasn't immediately swimming away from our canoe. For a second I felt sorry for Big Deddy, who was now just a shell of the fish he was just three minutes before. This went on for thirty seconds or so before he managed to swim away.

Mark and I looked at each other and laughed in amazement. Where is the video camera when you need it? We could have made *National Geographic,* the Discovery Channel, and been on *Larry King Live* if we would have caught this on film.

"Did you see that?" he asked.

"Yeah. The fish had one fin in the grave and didn't even know it."

"That's the most bizarre animal experience I've ever had."

"I'm with you, bro. People won't believe us, though."

"Hey. That bass was swimming with one side showing all bone. We both saw it."

My mind began to wander as Mark and I continued casting under the hot August sun. If fish could talk, what are Bill's (not his real name) pals saying to him down there as he swims by Charlie Catfish and Bobby Brim?

"Afternoon," says Billy Bass.

"Afternoon," responds Charlie Catfish, who, along with Bobby Brim, does a double take.

"Whoa! Did you see that? Ol' Billy looks like he ran into a prop or something," says a startled Bobby Brim.

"Yeah, I don't even think the poor guy knows he's missing half his body," says Charlie Catfish. "Oh well, I'm not going to be the one to break it to him."

"Me neither."

Now if fish could talk, that would be a BIG freak of nature. But you know, even if you heard them, no one would believe you. Think about it. What do you think that biblical writer who recorded the story of the talking donkey was thinking? Surely, he had just a moment of apprehension wondering what his family and friends would think about this story. The Red Sea parting is one thing. Here you have star power with the likes of Charlton Heston—I mean—Moses. But a donkey talking? *Of all the great and miraculous stories in the Bible, why do I have to be the one to get stuck with this one? Why couldn't I have written Exodus or Psalms? Now nobody's going to remember me, or if they do, they'll just laugh,* the writer must have thought.

Seriously, there are a lot of people walking around in this world who are half-fileted. Hurting people. The walking wounded, if you will. One of the main reasons followers of Christ are on this earth, it seems to me, is to reach out to those who are going through tough times or difficulty in their lives and be their friends. Oftentimes, I am afraid, we get so caught up in our own little world that we fail to see these folks. And they may be as close as our own family, coworker, or next-door neighbor.

Although for Billy Bass, well, his condition was terminal, I'm sad to say. Now before you question my comparison of a half-fileted bass to the human condition, remember what we learned about judging another's metaphors a couple of chapters back. Resist the urge.

Now, I trust you were moved reading about perhaps the only fish in the annals of marine life history who got half-fileted and yet swam away to tell about it.

Two Things to Remember

1. One of the best ways to be a witness for Christ is to demonstrate real care and concern toward people whose lives have been damaged for one or more reasons.

2. If you are a marine biologist, please don't write me and tell me we didn't see what we saw. The fish was swimming, I tell you.

Q. Did Adam Have a Navel?
Thomas Kinsey of Elmore, Tennessee

A. Thank you, Thomas, for this interesting question. This is indeed a mystery that has sent many a seminary student packing.

Before we attempt to answer this question we need to cover a little background material. First, who was Adam? Adam, of course, was the first human created by Almighty God and also the first human being who tried to pass the buck. Later President Harry Truman would make up for us guys with his famous, "The buck stops here," line, but Adam, he blamed Eve for his partaking of the forbidden fruit.

Now, as a general rule, what Adam did was perfectly normal and makes for a good marriage. Of course, I'm talking about doing whatever your wife tells you to do without question. I do this today as do most of my friends and we're cool with it. Adam did this and, well, his problem is pretty well summed up in one verse in Genesis chapter 3, verse 6, which reads:

"So when the woman saw that the tree was good for food, that it was pleasant to the eyes, and a tree desirable to make one wise, she took of its fruit and ate. *She also gave to her husband with her, and he ate*" (NKJV italics added).

Actually, Adam's problems began with *just one* sentence in one verse. One really *lousy* verse. Oh, would Adam take that verse back if only he could. One minute you're enjoying paradise in the heavenly hammock, seventy-five degrees, sunshine splashing down as a gentle breeze plays on your face, everything's great, your wife reaches over and says, "Here honey," and hands you a piece of fruit while you're only half paying attention. Maybe you've even got your eyes closed when you take a nice bite down and WHAM! The next thing you know, you've changed the plight of the human race for eternity.

This was a bad day in the life of Adam.

But did Adam have a navel? That was our question.

Answer: Really, I don't know, but since this is a book devoted to answering even the most trivial of questions—like this one from Thomas Kinsey of Elmore, Tennessee—I will give you my educated guess.

Thus after hours upon hours of tireless research, digging through Bible commentary after Bible commentary, and racking up one tremendous long-distance bill calling Greek scholars around the world, I have concluded two things. One, the Old Testament wasn't written in Greek. Many irate scholars, after asking where I got their numbers, told me this. Many with salty language. Secondly, I have to say that yes, Adam did have a "navel." I say "navel" in quotations because technically—where I come from anyway—this part of the anatomy is known as the belly button. So the correct way to phrase your question, Thomas, is: Did Adam have a belly button?

Answer, yes. No lint, however, would have been found in Adam's belly button until after the Fall since he was basically running around naked before then. The lint season—later added to the official Christian calendar—began soon after Adam donned the first fig leaf which, by the way, caused Adam much irritation and discomfort given that he didn't wear any underwear. At least, the Bible doesn't say anything about Adam having underwear.

Thomas, if you subscribe to the Adam Wore Fruit of the Looms theory—popular among some Mongolian monks back in the late 1960s—then please cite your biblical reference. It would seem to me any brand with the word "fruit" in it would not have been the briefs of choice by Adam given that he had already had one BIG-TIME bad experience with fruit.

Thank you for writing, Thomas, and you have a great day there in Elmore, Tennessee!

Is This Okay with God?

"You want to go with me?" Dad asked me.

"Yeah! Can I go?" I responded with childlike enthusiasm.

"Get your things together and we'll be leaving in the morning."

The year was 1977 and my dad, Don Wildmon, had just left the pulpit of First United Methodist Church in Southaven, Mississippi, to form what was then known as the National Federation for Decency (NFD). He had witnessed a moral decline in America and felt called by the Lord to do something about it. So he founded NFD (now called American Family Association).

One of the primary ways to grow an organization is by getting before people and convincing them you have a cause worth supporting. So in 1977, that's what Dad did. Yes, he traveled by plane some (when he could afford it or when an invitation included airfare), but most of the time, early on anyway, Dad got in his old green Buick and drove to his destination.

Sometimes, when school wasn't in progress, he would invite me to go along. For a kid fourteen years old, the idea of traveling to new parts of the country was very exciting. Also, I didn't like Dad traveling long distances alone. *It has to be lonely enough being a one-man organization,* I thought. And even at that age, I sensed that Dad needed some family support for his decision to leave the security of a nice church and blaze a trail into parts unknown.

So, Mom helped me pack a few items, and off Dad and I went to Atlanta, Georgia. From Southaven, just across the Tennessee state line from Memphis, this was about an eight-hour trip. I often carried games I could play by myself when we went on these journeys. Dad and I would talk about where we were going, what he would be doing, and finally about my favorite subjects—the St. Louis Cardinals and Mississippi State University sports. He didn't follow the Cardinals religiously like I did, but he did know enough about the Bulldogs to talk for a while. Mostly he just listened to me. I also remember how I would give him a strange look when some 1950s music would come on the radio. He would laugh and sometimes sing along. He knew these funny tunes. Then I would give him an even stranger look because, while Dad was a great preacher in my eyes, his singing left a whole lot to be desired. A whole lot. Still does. Sorry, Dad.

When we got to Atlanta we found this church. I can't remember what night of the week it was; I just know it was summertime in the Deep South and it was very hot and humid; the church had about 150 people packed in and the doors open in the back. It was also the first time I had ever been in a Pentecostal worship service with tambourines and all. I sat near the back as Dad delivered his message. Dad was very energetic behind the pulpit—as Methodists go anyway—and the shouts of "Amen!" and "Praise the Lord!" and, my personal favorite, "Come on!" did nothing but enhance his vigor. Dad, a lifelong Methodist, was right at home with our Pentecostal brothers and sisters. Me? The closest thing I had been exposed to that was anything like that worship service was at youth camp at Camp Lake Stephens. I remember singing without hymnals, moving around, being a little loud, hands lifted high. Why, this seemed like a. . .seemed like a. . .pep rally for a Mississippi State football game to me. *Can they do this in church?* I thought. *Is this okay with God?*

Looking back, I laugh about that night. Having been a Christian for many years now, I've found the saying true—I'm not sure who said it, but I believe it was the father of Methodism himself, John Wesley— "I would rather try to cool down a fanatic than try to warm up a corpse." These folks just loved Jesus and they were excited about Him. What's wrong with that? Nothing.

But what struck me that night in 1977, as much as anything, was that these folks were connecting with Dad's message. His sadness for the moral decline in

America was their sadness. His longing to try to do something about it was their longing. Dad said what the problems were and what—as he saw it in those days—the answers were: That if we were to have any hope for America, Christians—above all people—should rise up and be the salt and light Jesus says we should be in Matthew 5.

After the service the church gave him an offering. Many people gave him their home addresses and said, "Send me your newsletter; I want to support you, Brother Wildmon." And so the ministry grew and gained influence. I'm proud that my dad was willing to shun safety, security, and "respectability" to follow the Lord's calling so many years ago. There's no doubt in my mind that America's families are better off because people like Don Wildmon, Beverly LaHaye, James Dobson, Marlin Maddox, James Kennedy, Larry Burkett, and others chose to take a stand.

Nowadays, Dad and I rarely ride the highways together to far-off places so he can speak to groups. In fact, he doesn't travel or speak much anymore. After twenty years of beating that trail, one does tend to tire. But because of his early efforts we (AFA) now have supporters from many Christian denominations. The message for a better America where morality and virtue still matter still connects with hundreds of thousands of people of all different stripes.

Two Things to Remember

1. Christians need to hold high the biblical standard of right and wrong as defined in the Ten Commandments and the Sermon on the Mount.
2. Dad, bless his heart, still can't sing. And, sad to say, he passed this inability down to his eldest son.

CHICKEN

"Whatever you do, do it all for the glory of God," is what the Bible says (1 Corinthians 10:31 NIV). Even at work? Yes, I'm convinced even at work, no matter what your vocation may be.

One of the interests I have in meeting new people is to ask them what they do for a living. It takes all kinds to make this ol' world go around. I am most intrigued when I meet someone with an occupation that I know I could never do, no matter how much training I had.

Take air traffic controllers, for instance. Never. I'm the kind of guy who absolutely has to get up and go get some coffee several times during the workday. I just don't think I would work out in the tower.

"Yeah there, flight 407 or 704 or whatever your number is, just sit tight 'cause I got to run down the hall and get a cup of coffee. Might have to brew. Now, if you don't mind, why don't you just slow down a little—just a lil'—over Iowa so I don't lose you on my screen. In fact, I'm gonna put a yellow sticky right here where you are now and I'll catch up with you in a few minutes. Talk among yourselves."

I'd be afraid I'd get something in my eye at an inopportune moment, or that I might mistake a fly on the screen for a plane. And have you ever tried to understand a commercial pilot? These are very smart and talented people, but let's be honest, most sound half awake when they welcome you aboard—which is not a comforting feeling when you're already seated.

"Um, thank you ladies. . .flyin'. . .bumps. . .errr. . . any 'sistence. . .err. . .O'Hare 'round. . .err. . .relax. . ."

Passengers who actually care what the pilot says— mostly first-time flyers—look around at each other, shaking their heads, trying to put slurred or mumbled words together into understandable sentences. They don't want to be the one to disobey an order from the cockpit and cause the plane to crash. So they want to know what was growled lowly over the loudspeaker.

Every once in a while you get a pilot who can actually articulate and speak clearly in complete sentences. But more often than not, pilots on loudspeakers are like doctors writing prescriptions; you can't make heads or tails of it. I don't know which is more dangerous, a pilot who can't speak or a doctor who can't write.

Or how about mechanical engineers? Are you kidding me? In the first place I couldn't pass algebra, even if I were still taking it, and secondly, my mechanical skills end at the on-off button. And I can pump gas. But if it's not working at my house, don't look at me to fix it. My wife Alison told me to quit faking it a long time ago and I gladly obliged. I couldn't go on living a lie.

Once, when we were still newlyweds, she asked me about something having to do with our car's engine. The car was making a weird sound. Not wanting to let her know so soon in our happily ever after that I knew absolutely nothing about an automobile's engine—or engines in general, for that matter—I answered her, "Well, baby, it kind of sounds like the madulla oblongata to me."

"What?" Alison responded from the bedroom.

"Yeah, it's shaped real oblong with a gata jutting out the side. I'll see if I can't get one down at Auto Zone and put it in myself tomorrow," I bluffed. She called my bluff.

This next job I read about just about beats all I've ever heard. The story was out of a magazine called *AOPA Pilot*—obviously a publication for pilots. It read, and as Dave Barry would say, I'm not making this up:

"Learjet and an independent manufacturer of Learjet cockpit windshields are having a shootout, so to speak.

"When Perkins Aircraft of Fort Worth, Texas, offered the windshields at $10,000 less than the Learjet parts price last year, Learjet fired back with a service information letter warning customers that the windshields were not chicken tested. That is, the FAA did not require Perkins to prove that the windshields could survive a bird impact at approximately 300 knots (350 mph).

"To simulate the bird strike, Learjet tests its windows using a cannon that fires a chicken at 300 knots towards a stationary cockpit."

Now, think about this for a minute, ladies and gentlemen. Picture this if you will. No, really, go ahead and imagine this workstation.

I have a lot of questions here that beg to be asked.

In the first place, who builds these cannons that fire off the fowl? Cannons R Us? I mean, there can't be a great demand for these machines, can there? Did the folks at Learjet pick this baby up at a trade show of some kind after watching the demo? Are there chicken-launcher repairmen out there who go to school—like copier repairmen—to learn their trade and show up at the office every few days?

"How do, Bill?"

"Oh, pretty good. Yourself?"

"Not bad. Say, you think we need a new chicken launcher? This is the third time I've seen you out here this week. When's the warranty run out anyway?"

"Well, I've ordered a part from Angola, and once it comes in I think we can get you a few more miles out of that 1993 model. Although, I gotta tell you, and I'd get fired for saying this, but just between us boys, they just don't make chicken launchers like they used to, Tom. Why in the mid-eighties me and the Maytag repairman, we were tight. Always golfing and fishing.

Not anymore. Not since they started making these machines overseas."

Secondly, what qualifications do you need to operate a chicken launcher? Did Learjet interview twenty people before finally finding their man? Is there some institution of higher learning that gives a degree in chicken launching? Or did they just take Ed out of the mail room?

"Ed, we're moving you today to our new wing, so to speak. Your new position will be more of a challenge for you, Ed. We're confident you'll do just fine. Besides, this new job will be in one area so you won't have to be always running around like a chi. . . Well, you'll see what I mean."

And what does Ed tell folks when asked what he does for a living? What do his kids tell the other kids at school when asked what their daddy does for a living? Do schools take field trips to watch chicken launching?

Does Ed pull up his goggles, wipe his brow, and look down at his watch at about 11:30 anticipating lunch break? What does he think about as he loads one chicken after another? What does this machine sound like when it's clicking on all cylinders? I wonder, how do you know if you've had a good day or a bad day at work? Do you get stressed out? Do you ever go to KFC for lunch? Like I said, I've got a million questions.

The Bible says in Proverbs 16:3 that we are to commit our work to the Lord. Whatever it is that we do in life (including our vocation) as long as it's honest and moral, can be used by God to bring glory to Himself. I don't care what it is.

An honest day's work is a powerful witness to a boss that perhaps doesn't know the Lord. The boss and one's coworkers notice you going the extra mile without complaint. I know; I am a boss. Whatever it is that you do, do it as unto the Lord and that includes a good attitude. Even if it's chicken launching. Although, after an extensive check by the author, the Bible doesn't seem to address this particular vocation specifically.

Well, I don't have any answers to the perplexing questions I posed a couple paragraphs back. However, I think it's safe to say that this department will not be featured on any television advertisement, à la General Motors or Ford, showing Ed at work with the voice of James Earl "This is CNN" Jones saying: "Meet Learjet's Ed Walters, making your safety his first priority."

Two Things to Remember

1. Hard work and a positive attitude are good qualities for a Christian to display.
2. I called 146 colleges and universities and I could not find one school offering a degree in chicken launching. So I can't help you aspiring launchers. I would suggest you call Lear.

Tomorrow, I Love You

Have you seen the bumper sticker that reads, "Christians aren't perfect, just forgiven"? Well, along those lines, we Christians go through many of the same trials and difficulties that non-Christians do. We have good days and bad days just like anyone else. At least that's been my experience. But the big difference is we have Someone greater then ourselves to lean on when we go through difficulty.

Have you ever had one of *those* days? One of those days where nothing seems to go right? The kind of day when you get in the shower on a cold morning and realize your shampoo container is empty? The kind of day when you get to work only to realize one sock is black and the other tan? Or maybe one's brown and the other, well, there is no other sock. You were in a hurry and left it on the bathroom counter. The kind of day when you work on your computer for an hour, then hit the wrong key and your work is sent to never-never land? You know, a "ketchup-on-the-white-button-down-day." The kind of day when. . .well, you get the picture.

Recently, on one of my speaking engagement trips —this one to Vero Beach, Florida—I had one of those days when your patience is tested and you fight to maintain your Christian attitude.

My plane out of Memphis to Orlando through Atlanta departed at six A.M. so I decided to drive to Memphis and spend the night at a hotel. No problems yet, nor was I anticipating any. Checking out of the hotel, however, I guess I should have known it would be one of *those* days when the desk clerk helping me check out had an earring in her. . .well. . .it was in her nose. These are gaining popularity if you haven't noticed. I'm waiting for the first presidential candidate—in an attempt to attract the youth vote—to don one of these.

And while I'm on the subject, I'm just going to come right out and say it without regard for the book-purchasing power of nose-ringed Americans, but you folks, well, you look ridiculous wearing these hood ornaments. You do. You may be making a statement of individuality—which I'll grant you is your business—but you can absolutely forget—I say, FORGET—the insurance business.

There. I said it.

Now, I tried not to stare at this young lady, but I couldn't help myself. *Why would a person do this to herself?* I wondered nosily. This was somebody's daughter. How could she do this to her parents? While she was doing the paperwork and asking me light conversation questions about my stay, I'm tilting my head, staring at her nose ring, wanting to ask her if it was painful. It certainly looked painful.

As I walked away I was thinking to myself, *The day my daughter comes home with a nose ring is the day I'll consider my parenting a failure.* Perhaps I'll change that view later, but for now, that's the way I see it.

The nose-ring girl was to be a harbinger of things to come for me on that day. (And incidentally, I've been writing short stories for ten years now and this is the first time I've ever gotten to use the word "harbinger." So pardon my emotion. This is a literary milestone for me as an author. Okay, regain composure.)

Getting ready to board the plane, I picked up my suit and noticed, out of the corner of my eye, that my pants had fallen off the hanger. I checked to see how this had happened. A tiny screw had come loose and the hanger rung had fallen off, thus allowing my pants to slip off and onto the floor. If I had lost them, it would have been coat, tie, and wind-suit pants that evening. This might have worked in California. But in a community of mostly retirees in Florida. . .I don't think so.

I boarded the plane with the suit and, thank the Lord, none of the flight attendants had nose rings. Anyway, we arrived safe and on time in Atlanta. Awaiting my connecting flight to Orlando, I got the news every traveler hates to hear: "For those passengers awaiting flight 924 for Orlando, we have been informed it will be late arriving in Atlanta and so we have a new departing time of two P.M. Thank you for your understanding." Understanding is assumed when this happens. Next time this happens I'm going to go up to the counter and say, "Yes ma'am. Can you show me on my ticket here where I purchased some of this understanding you're talking about?"

Well, I had three hours leeway so this one and one-half hour delay isn't too big a deal, I thought. I had hoped to take a short walk on the beach but perhaps not now.

But instead of one and one-half hours late, the plane ended up two hours late leaving Atlanta. By the time I landed in Orlando I had started to feel a little pressure to get to Vero Beach on time. I still was okay, but I had to move along.

After quickly moving past the tourists to the car rental area, I walked up only to find my rental counter with a long, long line. None of the other rental companies had long lines, just mine.

So I waited and I waited and I waited until finally I made it up to where I was the next to be served. Why is it that when you're in this situation, there's always the couple at the desk ahead of you playing twenty-one questions with the clerk?

"Now, can you go over those directions with us once again and can you suggest a nice restaurant? And what about the beaches there; are the beaches nice and. . . ?"

And the friendly clerk responds, "Yes sir; do you prefer Italian, Mexican, Chinese. . . ?"

And there was this one man talking about his hometown with another desk clerk and the fact that she knew some people he knew and he knew some people she knew and. . .*come on, people, this isn't the coffee club! I've got to get my car and get out of here! In the immortal words of Sergeant Carter, "Move it! Move it! Move it!"* I thought.

Even with all my tough-luck traveling experiences, it still goes against my nature to be pushy, so I just sort of stood there looking at my watch, picking up my luggage and putting it down over and over, then sighing every minute or so while bobbing my head. Head-bobbing is important body language when you want to communicate frustration, you know. It also helps if you exhale loudly as your head drops. Then roll your eyes and throw up your hands—which is what I did—as you bob up. (Please, make a note of these traveling tips.) Finally, I did get my car and I was off to Vero Beach. And I do mean finally. Getting a car rental nowadays is like closing out on your home, twenty-three places to sign or initial. Honestly, I never even know what I sign half the time. They say initial, I initial. One day I'll probably get a notice that the loan I cosigned for with a car rental clerk in Dallas was defaulted on and now I owe $1 million.

Needless to say, I was going to be pushing it to meet my hostess, Joan McCorvey, at the hotel at 5:30. I hate the idea of someone waiting for me to get into town. So at this point I was driving under grace and not the law. (Just a little. Okay, so I was driving under a lot of grace and I realize this isn't a good example for you youngsters here, so just forget I even mentioned eighty-five miles an hour. Hey, at least I wasn't wearing a nose ring.)

You would think I could make it now with just one connecting interstate (I-95) to hit. But, no. No, no. Somehow I went into a black hole and missed the exit—to this day I don't know how this could have happened—for I-95. How does one miss an exit onto the most traveled interstate in the United States of America, you ask? Well, I don't know, but if it can be done, I'll do it. (Too close to the Bermuda Triangle, perhaps.) The next thing I know, I'm coming up to a stoplight. *Funny, I've never seen a stoplight in the middle of an interstate before,* I thought. *Wait a minute, this isn't the interstate!*

"Welcome to Cocoa Beach," the sign said.

"Cocoa Beach?" I yelled out, frustrated. *This is great!* I thought, trying to weave in and out of traffic to find my way back to I-95. From there, I pulled over and attempted a phone call to my host only to find my calling card not working properly. Mr. Murphy was right, ladies and gentlemen. So I phoned my secretary, Martha, and told her to call for me and I went back to find I-95. "Now if I go due west I have to run into I-95 sometime before I reach, say, California," I said to myself sarcastically. And you know it's a bad day when you start talking to yourself sarcastically. Finally, back on the right trail again, I make my way through the orange groves into Vero Beach.

Now, one of my weaknesses is the fact that I hate to shave. I always wait three days—sometimes four—or until I have to speak in public. It's a man's cross to bear, is the way I look at shaving. People are constantly asking me if I've got a part in our church pageant or if I'm growing a beard. My standard answer is, "I haven't decided yet." People understand indecision a lot better than they do laziness. But I had planned—and I do emphasize the word *planned*—on having ample time to shower and shave before meeting anyone in Vero Beach. Now that was in serious doubt and I had a three-day beard.

I prayed there would be a drugstore somewhere along the way to purchase a razor blade or else it would be a barbaric-looking vice president of American Family Association speaking to the annual banquet gathering for AFA Vero Beach.

It's now 5:25 P.M. According to the map I am near my hotel. *Thank You, Lord, there's a drugstore.* I run in, sprint over here and over there to find the razor blades and dash to the front counter. One man and a couple in line ahead of me. I pleaded with the guy—perhaps my age—about to check out, "Do you mind if I cut in line? I'm running late for a very important speaking engagement."

As I panted, he looked at me stone-faced and said sternly, "Yes, I do." My shoulders dropped. Nine out of ten people are understanding in this situation—not this dude.

"Okay," I replied in disbelief as thoughts from my darker side danced through my head. I wanted to slap him, I did. But I didn't have time to engage in what might follow. I also didn't think it would be good public relations for me (or the group I was speaking to) for me to get arrested—and the guy was much bigger than me. Still, he was a jerk. The couple behind him were very nice and I went ahead, paid, and ran back to the car.

For you Floridians, I got behind Mr. First-Come-First-Serve on the road and, for the record, he was not from the Sunshine State. While driving—I must confess—I had to deal with a strong urge to ram his car from behind. But I didn't. Instead, I looked for my hotel.

According to my map I should have seen it by now. No hotel. I kept driving until I came upon the city limits sign. As I turned around I came up beside a local stopped at a red light and honked, motioned for him to roll down his window, and asked directions (the ultimate act of male humility) to the hotel. Fortunately it wasn't one of those, "Go three blocks take a right, go 1.2 miles on Jackson, then make a U-turn back a half a mile until you get to Sam's restaurant. Go through the back of Sam's parking lot, take a sharp left onto Gibson, and the hotel will be five blocks on your left. I think. That's if you're traveling south. If you're going north you might miss the sign because it's off the road a little and. . ." We've all had these directions given to us by well-meaning locals, haven't we? And we shake our head "yes" the whole time, knowing we haven't any idea what we're supposed to do after that first right. Or was it a left?

Fortunately, I got some easy directions and as I drove into the hotel registration area, I saw what the problem was. The hotel was in the very act of changing signs. I'm talking guys out there pulling ropes up, taking down the old sign, and getting ready to put up a new one. Honestly.

Joan was waiting. I told her I was sorry, checked in, quickly shaved (one cut), threw on my suit (pants and all) and made the banquet. The people were great, everything went well, and I was taken back to the hotel after the banquet. Wow, what a day! A day to forget (with the exception of the banquet). I didn't even get to see the beach except just for a minute or two as I drove away the next morning.

Now I realize this was one day of minor difficulty in the life of one small person on this huge globe. But it's comforting to know that when things aren't going well, when you're having problems in your life or people have done you wrong, there's always another day. There's always tomorrow.

You know, our Christian walk is sometimes like this. We have bad days for one reason or another. We have bad seasons in our lives. Perhaps it's due to something we've done or perhaps it's for reasons we don't understand. Nevertheless, God is the God of a second chance. The God we serve is the Lord of tomorrows and second chances. And thirds. And many more for sinners like me, bless His holy name. He forgives, He helps us get up when we fall, and He restores us when we need restoration. He is our Rock in times of trouble. Thank You, Lord, that You never change.

Now Lord, help me forgive that. . .umm. . .child whom You love who wouldn't let me cut line.

Two Things to Remember

1. The Lord is with His children in the good times and the bad. Our circumstances do not effect His faithfulness to walk with us.
2. If you wear a nose ring, I invite you to write nosy ol' me and tell me why you do so and what your career opportunities are. Just wondering.

COMES AROUND

What goes around, comes around. I've heard that my whole life. So have you. Somebody, somewhere back there, thought this a truism and so it caught on. It may have been C.S. Lewis who first came up with this saying. But then again, maybe not. Quite frankly, I'm tired of seeing C.S. Lewis quoted in every Christian book on the market. Aren't you? Got a book on the Bible and gardening; guess who they quote? C.S. Lewis. Got a Christian book on shoveling horse manure; guess who's quoted? Why, C.S. Lewis, of course. I'll bet if C.S. could come back from the dead and say one thing, he would say this: "Hey! Quit quoting me so much. I never said half of those things anyway."

The first time I remember hearing this saying—what goes around, comes around—was in Little League when Jay Miller went to bat with the game on the line for our team sponsored by the Tupelo Bank Association. That's what was on the front of our green jerseys. Bank Association. Other teams, I seem to remember, had real aggressive names like Tigers, Lions, and

Bulldogs. Not my team. We were the Bank Association. Strikes fear in your heart, doesn't it?

Not only did we have a boring name, but back in the early seventies Little League teams only played five innings. Times were tough and President Nixon said we had an energy crisis, so we all pitched in to help save America by playing only five innings instead of the customary nine. Maybe it had something to do with the lights staying on at the fields too long; I don't know. All I know is, I felt cheated, even if we were saving America.

Jay Miller came up to bat with two out, bases loaded, the tying run on third and the winning run on second. The rest of us sat in the dugout, just staring out at the drama unfolding on Andy Reese Field, secretly thankful it was Jay out there with the game in the balance and not us. Not that Jay was a great player by any means, about average, as I recall, but we were just glad the weight of winning and losing was on his small shoulders and not ours. Swing and miss. Strike one. Duck back, ball goes over the plate, strike two. The next ball is way high; I'm talking about six inches over his head, but Jay Miller swings anyway, his eyes closed, just hoping and praying to make some type of contact so he wouldn't be the goat. Everybody's staring; Jay's mom closes her eyes too. No chance. Strike three. Jay Goat is out to pasture and he looked bad doing it.

Poor Jay. We lost and it was all his fault. None of that postgame "team" psychology stuff works at this point. Maybe in football, where your teammate failed to throw a block for you, but not in baseball. In baseball it's just you and the pitcher. Man-to-man. And Jay lost the game. He knew it, we knew it, his mother knew it, the coach knew it—everybody knew it.

After we did the traditional "good game" hand slaps with the opposing team, Coach Chris Moore gathered us around as he did after every game and gave us the good, bad, and ugly from his perspective. There was a little grumbling from some of my teammates who couldn't believe Miller struck out on three pitches. Mostly Coach was positive and instructive, saving his rare criticisms for loafing and inattention. But I remember after this particular game, the game Jay Miller lost for us, he looked around, motioned for Jay to come up front, then backed away, leaving Jay in the spotlight and said, "Jay, you idiot! What were you trying to do with that last swing, bring rain? You lost the game! You! All by yourself! You're a loser, Miller, face it! Now go sit down!"

Shocked, are you? Well, I would have been too if that had really happened. But you should know me well enough by now to know *I'm just kidding*. He said no such thing. What Coach actually said was perfect: "Now, boys, we had a lot of opportunities to win this ball game. In the third inning, we had the bases loaded and nobody out and couldn't get a hit. In the fourth inning we made three errors on routine plays and it cost us four runs. Then in the fifth, we couldn't get a hit."

Then he turned to Jay Miller, who had lost the game for us, the Bank Association, and said, "Jay, don't you worry about that last at bat. You'll get 'em next time, buddy. Guys, next time it could be you up to bat with the game on the line, so don't blame Jay or any of your teammates for this loss. We win as a team and we lose as a team. Remember this, what goes around, comes around."

Feeling kind of guilty for thinking ill of Jay, myself, although I didn't verbalize it, I went up and hit his glove with mine. This was okay for eleven-year-old males to do in 1974. Basically, you were saying, "I like you" without getting all mushy. I said to Miller, "It's like Coach said, Jay, what goes around comes up and down, man. Wasn't that it? Anyway, it's not important. The important thing is next time it could be me up to bat and I might lose the game for us just like you did tonight. So don't worry about it. Wanna go get a snow cone?"

My life as a therapist began and ended that night. Jay, man, he went home with his mom, in tears. I guess I made things worse while trying to help. As Jay got in the car and his mom closed the back door, kind of in my face, I wondered what I'd said wrong. Maybe they were members of some off-brand church that didn't believe in snow cones or something. Oh, well.

What goes around, comes around means, for me, anyway, is that we need to have understanding and compassion for our fellowmen when they're going through difficult times—because one day it might very well be us whom life has soured on. Perhaps we've done something to mess up, or maybe troubling circumstances have developed for reasons we don't understand. In any case, I think this is what Jesus was talking about when He gave us the Golden Rule. We are to do unto others as we would want others to do unto us.

A few years ago I had an opportunity to do a better job of applying the Golden Rule than I had done with Jay Miller.

My brother-in-law Neal Clement and his two little boys, Neal Russell, age four, and Drew, age two, along with four members of our family, Alison, me, Wesley, age eight, and Walker, age three, took Neal's boat up to Bay Springs Lake in the northeastern part of Mississippi one Sunday afternoon. . . . Oops! Did I say Sunday afternoon when there was something going on at the church Sunday evening and there was absolutely no way we could get back in time for it if we went skiing at Bay Springs? I obviously am not remembering correctly. This must have been a "nobody-at-church-at-all-except-maybe-the janitor" Saturday afternoon. Yep. Now that I think about it, it was most certainly Saturday, so save your letters.

Neal had a very nice new ski boat. We loaded everything we needed on the boat, ready for a fun-filled afternoon on the water and guess what? The battery was dead. On this new boat. "How could this have happened?" we adults questioned. Neal guessed

Donna, my sister who wasn't with us, had let the little boys play in the boat at home and they had turned on something which drained the battery. So Neal went over to the marina and came back fifteen minutes later with the mechanic who jump-started the battery.

"You better run it awhile so it'll charge up," advised this gentleman.

"Oh, we sure will," said Neal. "We just appreciate you coming over here and giving us a hand."

"No problem."

We took off for the open water. I love to sit up front and let the wind hit my face on a sunny summer afternoon. We ran the boat fifteen minutes before we found a good place to let the kids tube. Neal reemphasized to Alison and I—the other adults—that we needed to let the motor run thus allowing the battery to charge.

"Whatever you do, don't cut off the engine," he said as he attached the rope to the tube. No sooner had Neal said those words than he did it. He being Neal Russell Clement, the four-year-old son of my sister Donna and the man who had just said, "Whatever you do, don't cut off the engine," walked by the wheel, reached over, and turned the key. Silence. We didn't really think about one of the kids taking it upon themselves to turn off the boat. Alison, Neal, and I looked at each other in disbelief, hoping it would restart.

"Try it, Neal," I said. "I think we ran it long enough."

Neal then turns the key and guess what? Nothing happens. Neal tries it again. Again, nothing happens. Our stomachs knot up. Here I entered denial in a serious way.

"Try it again, Neal," I said.

"It's not doing anything, Tim."

"Try it again, Neal."

"Tim, he's tried it; it's not even turning over," said Alison.

"Try it again, Neal," I continued.

"Daddy, it's not starting, do you see?" said Wesley.

"Try it again, Neal."

In case you need a word picture, ladies and gentlemen, boys and girls, we are out in the middle of a huge lake with four children and no HORSEPOWER.

"We're just gonna have to wave down a boat," Alison said.

"Try it again, Neal," I said.

"Would you quit it and help me flag down a boat!"

For about thirty minutes we waved and waved. A lot of people waved back. Friendly, but not helpful. From 200 yards I suppose it's hard to distinguish a "Party-on dude" motion from a "Please help us we're dying here!" motion. Finally, a couple of guys on jet skis came over. They tried to jump-start us but it didn't work. Neal asked if he could borrow one of the jet skis and took off for help in the mainstream where all the boats were speeding by. Basically, he looked like a rodeo cowboy roping a calf as he ran up beside this one boat trying to get it to stop long enough to explain our situation. Finally, the folks followed Neal to our boat and offered assistance. It was Charlie Miller and his family. As we talked we soon learned they were from Tupelo and we had mutual friends. For some reason, he couldn't jump-start us either. What now? Now, we use the ski ropes for a towline, that's what.

It took them forty long minutes to tow us back to the boat ramp. We felt so bad about ruining their day, but they didn't seem to mind at all. They were just glad to help out. Neal offered Charlie money, but he wouldn't take it.

"How can I ever repay you?" asked Neal.

"Help somebody else out who's in need sometime," replied Charlie. "That's how you can repay us."

"Hey, I will," said Neal. "You can bet that I will."

I vowed the same.

Well, as the Lord would have it, it wasn't a week later in the Wolfchase Galleria parking lot in Memphis that our family had an opportunity to help a family in the same situation. Granted they weren't stranded out on the open water, but it was still a young woman with four children and her car wouldn't start.

It was night and Alison was getting something in the mall. The young woman walked over, a few feet from my car, and motioned for me to roll down my window. She then told me of her situation and I told her I'd be glad to help out. We tried to jump-start her battery but as it turned out—after twenty minutes or so of trying to jump-start her car—it was her alternator. Alison figured this out. I don't believe in alternators. I don't think there is such a part on a car. I think this is what people say when they don't know what's really wrong with an automobile. Have you noticed this? Especially men use the mythical "alternator" as a catchall for anything that keeps a car from running. I can hear it now. . .

"What's wrong with the car, honey?"

"I don't know."

"Could it have something to do with the fact that the gas gauge says empty?"

"Oh no, couldn't be that simple. Must be the alternator."

We waited with her as she got in touch with her husband and he came from across town.

"Thank you so much," she told our family. "I felt so alone." By this time our kids had made friends with her kids. They were black, ours white. You read that right. White Southerners lending a hand to a black family? Imagine that? (Please excuse the sarcasm here. It's just that I tire of the Hollywood stereotyping of white Southern males as racist.)

Bottom line, I have preached the virtue of helping others to my kids many times. I've read them Bible story after Bible story. We've practiced extending care and concern within the safe, sterile confines of our own family and church. However, here my three children, within a week's time, got to live out—both receiving and giving—what I had been trying to teach them with people different from us in many ways and whom we didn't even know. And it felt good. Very good.

Indeed, C.S. Lewis was right. What goes around, comes around.

Now, excuse me.

Say, Neal, try it one more time, would ya?

Two Things to Remember

1. Jesus said in Matthew 22:39, "You shall love your neighbor as yourself" (NKJV).
2. Some deep philosophy here. . . In addition to "what goes around, comes around," it is also true that whatever goes up must also come down—in a roundabout way. Think about it. And don't say I didn't warn you.

Q. Why Did David Choose Five Smooth Stones When It Only Took One to Kill Goliath?

Kenneth Lobotomy of Hattfield, Ohio

A. **Excellent question,** Kenneth. Just excellent, my friend. My staff will now enter your name in our big shoebox here at our offices in Tupelo, Mississippi. You will be eligible for our drawing to win an all-expenses trip (including bus fare, tent, and snack food) to the beautiful and cozy little town of International Falls, Minnesota. A village that does more advertising on the Weather Channel than Royal Caribbean. Now the drawing will be held next July, but the trip will not actually be until January. So save that Christmas bonus, Mr. Lobotomy, you just may be spending the New Year in the Land of Ten Thousand (Frozen) Lakes.

Now to your question: Why did David choose five smooth stones when it only took one to kill Goliath? The first thing I would like to do here, Kenneth, is spend a few minutes talking about Goliath. To some extent I have to feel sorry for the guy; I'll be honest. In his unauthorized (due to the fact none of Goliath's family could be reached to sign a book deal) biography *The Goliath We Never Knew,* best-selling author John Grisham writes about Goliath's early years:

"Goliath was born on or about the month of April or September with his elbow halfway up his arm. We don't really know what year, but we do know it preceded the births of David Brinkley and David Letterman. He was forty-two inches long at birth which caused the startled OB-GYN to yell at his mother, 'My word, lady, you've had a circus freak!'

"When Goliath entered kindergarten he was six-feet, five-inches tall and weighed 275 pounds. It was about this time that Alabama, Penn State, and Notre Dame began recruiting young Goliath, offering him a scholarship to play the entire offensive or defensive lines, whichever he wanted. In the fourth grade he stood eight feet tall and weighed 450 pounds. He stood many, many heads and many, many shoulders above the other kids. He felt awkward and the other kids teased him relentlessly about his height, clothing, and the fact that Goliath was always hitting his head on the ceiling fan in math class. 'Expecting a flood there, Goliath?' they would joke about his 'high water' pants which exposed his white athletic socks. 'How's the weather up there?' others would say when the clouds were low, knowing young Goliath couldn't see down to fight back. This built up an understandable anger and rage inside young Goliath. An anger that he would later use to his advantage on the battlefield." (Grisham went on to write another paragraph or two in this book, threw in a couple of underdog lawyers, and it, too, shot to the top of the *New York Times'* best-seller list.)

Kenneth, I really believe that little David knew some of what Goliath had been through and sympathized, given the fact that he was always known in his family as "little runt" and basically told to watch the sheep and "get lost" by his brothers and schoolmates. David put himself, figuratively, of course, in Goliath's sandals and asked himself: "If I were going to get nailed between the eyes with a rock that would kill me, would I want a rough, jagged rock to pierce my flesh, or would I prefer a smooth, slick stone?" The answer was obvious to David. He was already going to smote and behead Goliath; "Why add insult to injury?" he said to himself.

Why five stones though? Why not just pick up one out of the creek? Well, some theologians who watch a lot of *Andy Griffith* reruns believe that David liked to skip rocks on the water (much like Opie). Their theory is David didn't want to pass up the opportunity at four nice, sleek, slick stones which he could probably use to break his own personal record of eight skips set back in A Long Time Ago, B.C.

Other off-the-wall Bible scholars say David planned to use the other four stones to get back at his big brothers for pickin' on him for all those years.

David decided to teach them a lesson they would never forget when they bent over to pick up the soap in the river. The Bible, however, as is often the case, is silent on this issue, Kenneth, so we are left to our own educated imaginations—some of which run wild with crazy and bizarre speculation based on absolutely nothing, the likes of which you will never find in a hard-facts-only book like the one you are now reading.

Aren't you glad you asked now, Kenneth? You have my permission to use my answer in Sunday school class. Just make sure you credit Billy Graham, Pat Roberston, or some other Christian leader or teacher, as I prefer my reward when I get to heaven.

OF MICE AND ME

Fear. It can make people do strange things. And
embarrassing things. I'll explain in a few moments.

I remember begging and pleading with my parents
to let me go see *Jaws* at the local theater. They said
"no," it wouldn't be good for me. But I whined and I
bugged and I pestered. I kept on and kept on. It was
rare that I wore my parents down on anything because
usually they put a halt to the asking, but this time, for
some reason, I got to them. Mom relented—in a moment of weakness—and gave me a "well, I guess so"
answer that parents give sometimes. I know how this is
as a father of three children myself now. You let your
kids do something that's really against your better
judgment because you're tired or because you've said
"no" ten consecutive times and you think maybe you're
becoming too overbearing and it's time to say "okay."

Well, I went to see *Jaws*. I watched the Great
White Shark rip to pieces and devour several un-
suspecting people who, in retrospect, should have
KNOWN something really BAD was about to happen

to them just by that awful, pulsating music that began playing just before each attack. *Get a clue, people!* I remember thinking before each shark attack, *Get out of the water, you idiot! Don't you know that music means you're about to be dinner?*

You know what? Those stupid people in the movie never learned anything from the dreadful sound of that music, but I certainly did. What I learned was, my parents were right. The movie scared me to death. When I got home that night I couldn't go to sleep; I tossed and turned. All I could see when I shut my eyes was that shark eating people alive, knowing that the next day I was supposed to go swimming with Rusty Wilkinson. And before that I would probably have to get a bath. Even the bathtub seemed daunting after *Jaws*. Laugh if you will, but those who saw the movie in the mid-seventies understand. I cried and asked Mom to come into my room. I was twelve at the time.

"Mama, you were right," I said as I held her tight. "Please don't ever let me go to another movie like that again. I can't put it out of my mind."

Mama reminded me, in her soft, sweet voice, how she had warned me about the movie for a reason and how movies and television shows can make lasting impressions on young minds. Then she prayed with me, left the door open with the hall light on, told me I could come in her room if I got frightened in the night, and promised she wouldn't tell any of my friends I was a scaredy-cat. This is why little boys love their mamas.

But Mama was right about movies having lasting impressions. Even to this day, I have such a healthy respect for sharks that I give them plenty of space. When our family makes our annual trek to Hilton Head Island each May, I take the villa and beach, giving Mr. Shark the ENTIRE ocean in which to frolic and enjoy a buffet of tasty items other than my legs. But my wife, Alison, while she's no fan of sharks either, still ventures out into the ocean just a little—maybe up to her waist—as she enjoys the waves. However, as brave as Alison is, ironically, it's a diminutive land creature that strikes terror in the heart of my wife. What diminutive land creature, you ask? Assuming you know what diminutive means, you are probably thinking snakes, right? Good guess and she does hate snakes, but that's not the worst. She also hates lizards but we don't have too many of them around our area. What makes my Alison—who is a "get-out-my-way-mister-I-can-handle-it-fine-by-myself" type if there ever was one—tremble and call me home from work is an animal commonly known as the—are you ready for this—field mouse. That's right. The harmless, tiny field mouse—who probably couldn't whip a cricket if his life depended on it—is an imposing and intimidating foe for Al, who can handily run off three pit bulls from our yard with just a broom and the traditional Southern "Getonouttaheah dawg!" yell. (If you're not from the South, please have someone who is shout "getonouttaheah" for you. This is yet another expansion of the English language that we Southerners think all of America would find useful, especially when confronting unwanted members of the canine family. If pronounced properly with correct body language, it works every time and is much more effective than "shoo, dog," which is also used in many parts of North America.)

The first house Alison and I built was in a field about three miles out of Tupelo on a country road. We had a few other houses around us, but none very close. The only people that could really see what we were doing around our place were Mark and Carla Jarrett. Nice people, they were. One evening as we were winding down for bed, Alison went back up to the kitchen to sweep or something while I was gathering the latest sports news on CNN. That's one of my chores, keeping up with the world of sports. As they say, tough job, but somebody's got to do it. Alison depends on me to inform her on who's number one. As I lay on our bed watching TV, I thought I heard Alison saying something directed probably toward me since Wriley and Wesley were already asleep. I remember it went something like this, "TIM, WOULD YOU GET UP HERE NOW! THERE'S SOMETHING IN OUR GARBAGE CAN!"

This always happens, doesn't it, men? Nick Charles is just about to announce the one score I really care about and now my wife is yelling about something in the trash can. So, I wait just a minute. Go ahead and admit it, fellas, you do it too. "C'mon, Nick, give me the score," I say to myself as I pull back the sheets and crawl out of bed. *Why now? I already had my spot all warm,* I think to myself.

"Now, Nick, now!" I raise my voice at the TV set.

"TIM, GET UP HERE NOW!"

Forget you, Nick, you loser. So I walk up front in my briefs, nothing else. (There's a reason why I'm getting so personal, so stay with me.)

"What in the world are you doing?" I ask Alison when I see that she's atop our dryer.

"There are mice or something in our garbage can; listen."

She was right; there was something crawling around in our plastic container.

"Get them out, take them out, get those good-for-nothin' dirty, disease-ridden animals out of my house now!" Alison told me emphatically.

"Just what exactly are you trying to say, baby? Are you saying you don't want these lil' cute wouldn't-hurt-a-flea critters out of our warm house into the dark, cold night where large cats are on the prowl looking to pounce and crush their tiny heads, drag them away, and have them for dinner?"

So I opened the door underneath the sink, pulled the trash can out, and looked inside. Just as I suspected. There were three mice trying desperately to scale the twenty-four-inch container. They had obviously been running along the pipes and fallen in.

"Al, do you remember that nursery rhyme? How'd

that go, now? Something about three blind mice, see how they nibble your toes off a little at a time or. . ."

"Tim, this is not a time for jokes. Now take the mice outside, WAY away from the house and get rid of them," she said.

So I picked up the light plastic container which had nothing else in it and went out the kitchen door to our carport. Now it was about 10:30 P.M. and very dark outside. So the fact that I was in my underwear didn't really concern me. Yes, the Jarretts could perhaps see me if they cared to, but I knew Mark was watching the sports report that I was now missing and Carla was not going to be standing at the window waiting on one of the Wildmons to come out at 10:30 at night. There was the occasional car that went racing by at sixty miles an hour. But as I say, these things don't really enter a man's mind when all he has to do is walk out of his house 100 feet or so, in the dark, and dump out three mice that have paralyzed his wife, and return to the house. No problem, right?

Well, not wanting to walk out into the grass and dirt, I simply made my way down the concrete driveway about 100 feet. And just as I got ready to dump the little varmints out, my lovely and talented wife—who has many, many great qualities—decided she had better check on her Knight Without Shining Armor and see how I was making out. In order to do so, she wanted to see me. So what did she do? Yes, she did. She flipped the switch. The switch that controlled the two floodlights that make our driveway light up like a high school football field on a Friday night!

"How ya doin' out there, hon?" Alison asked as I stood there, in my briefs, blinded as I turned around to look back at her.

"Oh, I don't know, baby; you tell me since you can see!" I responded in disbelief as a car slowly drove by the front of our house.

"Oh, I'm sorry," she said as she turned off the lights, realizing that her husband, deacon at First Evangelical Church and vice president of American Family Association, was on exhibit as "The Man in Underwear Who Walks Around His Driveway with a Garbage Can in His Hand Late at Night."

Whoever you were out there who witnessed this, there is a reasonable explanation for what appeared to be A Man in Underwear Who Walks Around His Driveway with a Garbage Can in His Hand Late at Night. You may disagree with my decision to go outside without any *real* clothes on, but please understand there is context here. I absolutely beg you not to start any rumors or stories that might cast a shadow on my reputation as someone who generally wears clothes when outdoors and who generally doesn't engage in any bizarre pagan rituals in his driveway late at night. And I do not drink alcoholic beverages. Please believe me; I was sober when I went out in my drawers to get rid of the mice. On second thought, maybe that's not such a good confession.

So now you know the truth. I am scared of sharks and Alison is frightened—no, petrified—of mice. But there are many people who live in constant fear. Perhaps you know someone like this. They let it dominate their lives. I know people who are always worried that they are going to get some dreaded disease. Then there are people who don't attempt a whole lot in life because they are consumed with a fear of failure. Many folks fear confrontation and avoid it at all cost. It would be much healthier, though, for them to deal with whatever the person or problem is that they are avoiding. Confrontation involving other people, if handled in the right spirit, is most often not nearly as bad as you might think it would be.

Well, as I said earlier, fear can cause otherwise sane people to do some crazy things. The Bible says God has not given us a spirit of fear. In fact, the Lord gives His children quite the opposite. He imparts to us faith, peace, and contentment. You don't have to live in bondage to fear. If you are in this situation, I would encourage you to pray and read the Bible often. I would also encourage you to surround yourself with friends who can help you overcome your anxieties. Sure, we all experience fear sometimes. It's only natural. But as believers we have the right to control it and not allow fearful thoughts or circumstances to control us.

Now, I don't know why I didn't at least slip some shorts on. You know, it's just one of those "spur of the moment" guy things. If it seems unnecessary—then most likely, ladies—we're not gonna do it. But of course, this wouldn't have been a problem if someone of the OPPOSITE SEX, who will go unnamed here, hadn't turned the floodlights on her near-naked husband.

Two Things to Remember

1. The Bible says in 2 Timothy 1:7: "For God has not given us a spirit of fear, but of power and of love and of a sound mind" (NKJV). We don't have to let fear dominate our life.
2. What's the deal with you ladies and mice? It's seems the smaller the critter is, the more frightened you become. Grow up. Hey, what's that noise? Over there by the window. . .

VACATION OBSERVATIONS

For the first time in a long time, our entire family got away for a vacation the first week in August a couple of years ago.

When are we going to get there, Dad?

My dad, mom, brother, sister, my other sister, her husband, their then two-year-old, and my gang, consisting of Alison, me, and our three model children, ages seven, six, and twenty-two months, made the trip. Twelve people, two cars, and a van. No pets. We loaded up and drove from Tupelo, through Memphis, across the mighty Mississippi, and through Arkansas to the beautiful Lake of the Ozarks in central Missouri at the invitation of some longtime friends, Dick and Sherly Bott, who own a very nice place there. And it was free. It was a wonderful and relaxing few days.

When are we going to get there, Dad?

My favorite vacations are those where you get away with the family somewhere quite removed from the routine of everyday living, where the lodging is cool, comfortable and—best of all—free. I like free a lot. Do

I feel guilty about taking advantage of friends? Absolutely not. If God had intended us to feel guilty about taking advantage of friends, or family for that matter, He would have put a commandment in the Bible somewhere that read: "Thou shalt feel guilty—at least a little bit—about taking advantage of friends." I can't find anything like that in the Scriptures. What are friends for if not to be used and abused? They use and abuse me.

When I was a kid I couldn't for the life of me understand why my parents were basically old fogies when it came to vacations. I mean, they actually wanted to rest and relax. When the four of us kids went out to the beach, Mom and Dad just wanted to watch from a chair by the pool or stay in the hotel room and read. *How boring,* I used to think. *These poor people have no life. Reading is for school, not vacation.* And like true American parents, they also threatened to turn around and go home every two hours or so—whenever an uprising in the station wagon would occur. However, you start catching on to this bluff after eight hours of driving and four empty threats. *Dad's not going to turn around and go home now, it would be a huge waste of gas,* I used to think to myself. But I didn't dare say it.

Usually it was my two sisters, Angela and Donna, who got into it over such emotional issues as what Barbie would wear between Mobile, Alabama, and Ft. Walton Beach, Florida. Me, I basically played the role of Switzerland and stayed neutral during these disputes. I guess I could have weighed in with an opinion on Barbie's attire, but I don't know; I never could work up any passion about plastic dolls the way I did about *really* important stuff such as baseball.

Well, now being on the other end of things, I know why my parents were less excited about the sights and sounds of a particular vacation destination and more excited about the lounge chairs or the view from the deck or what steak house to eat at that night.

When are we going to get there, Dad?

When our family of five finally arrived at the Lake of the Ozarks, Alison and I got unloaded, said hello to the Botts and told them we would be out of our cabin in a couple of hours to join them. Since we were tired from the drive, first we wanted to take a nap. They said to rest as long as we wanted and left us alone. Whew! Where's the couch?

Wrong.

My daughter—with her younger brother nodding "that's right"—said, looking up at me, "Nap! Are you kiddin' us, Dad? We drove all this way, we're finally here, we've got the lake in our front yard, and you and Mom want to nap? I am not believing this! Do you believe this, Wes?"

Wesley nodded in the negative.

Without warning, I had a mutiny on my hands.

While Wriley mouthed and Wesley head-bobbed in agreement, they shed their clothes down to the bathing suits they had worn underneath since they'd dressed earlier in the morning (perhaps since we had left Tupelo the day before, I really don't know). They were ready for the sun and fun.

Okay. Try a little reason.

"Yeah, I thought since we've been driving for so long we might lie down and rest a while," I said as I flashed back to my childhood. The concept—once very unreasonable and fun-killing when my parents presented it—seemed totally reasonable now. (Just a point of fact—WE didn't drive all the way—I did.)

Reason didn't work. So, I decided I didn't need a nap after all and went swimming with the kids. Some hills you die on, others you just shrug your shoulders on. This was a shrugger.

What is it about the relationship between parents and their children? Why is it that most of us will do anything for our kids? By "anything" I mean that when we have children we spend the better part of twenty years trying to make them happy. You can't really appreciate this question, I suppose, unless you have or have had kids. What makes our love run so deep for our flesh and blood?

One of the most special memories I have of Christmases gone by was in 1974. I was eleven years old. Dad was a Methodist pastor of a small church, so we didn't have much money. In fact, we were poor. Yeah, that's it, we were poor folk. Those were tough times, 1974. We had an energy crisis and all. And when I walked to school I walked barefooted ten miles. Yeah, that's it, ten miles barefooted. Uphill. Both ways. Times were tough back in 1974. Then there was the war. I've forgotten what the war was about or whom we fought, but times were tough for barefooted boys who had to walk ten miles to school uphill both ways and I'm sure we had kind of war going on. In fact, times were so tough, I remember President Nixon coming on television to tell the country to, "Ask not what your country can do for you, but what you can do for your country." Then he told us to, "Go and sin no more." Times were tough, I tell you. Sometimes even presidents had a difficult time coming up with something original and often used quotes out of context, mixing them together incoherently, leaving many Americans scratching their heads wondering what on Earth they were supposed to do with this information. Then came Watergate, and we don't even want to get into that. Then Elvis died and our country never has been quite the same since. Tough times, the mid-seventies.

Now where were we? (Had to get one of those hard-times stories in for posterity.) Oh yes. For Christmas 1974 my dad gave each of his children a very special gift. The gifts were placed in very small boxes that we each pulled out from under the tree on Christmas morning. My first reaction—although I didn't say anything—was disappointment. How could anything fun come from such a small container? When I tore off the wrapping paper and opened the box there was nothing shiny. There was nothing that looked like a game. All

I saw were a few slips of paper, which I promptly looked under. Maybe there was some money. No, no money either. As I looked up at Dad perplexed he told me to read the slips of paper. I looked back down and pulled them, one at a time, from the box.

"Good for one free milk shake, you and I."

"Good for a father-and-son trip to see the Mississippi State vs. Kentucky basketball game."

"Good for a weekend fishing trip together on the Tennessee River."

"Good for four hours to do whatever you want to do."

Wow! I thought. This was too good to be true.

"Are you serious?" I asked Dad.

"Absolutely," he responded. "I want you and me to spend more time together."

I received many Christmas gifts from my parents over the years. Very few do I remember. However, I will never forget the best gifts—the gifts of time, attention, and love—came in the simplest of boxes. And those little slips of paper are still the best gifts I've ever received for Christmas. I will never, ever forget what Dad communicated to me that day with those little pieces of paper.

Now it's my turn.

When are we going to get there, Dad?

I don't know, kids, but cherish the journey.

Two Things to Remember

1. Time is a commodity given to us by God. As parents we need to use it wisely.
2. My, how the definition of the word "vacation" changes from childhood to adulthood. Give me a lounge chair by the beach and a cold glass of ice tea.

CHRISTIAN FAMILY? (YOU DECIDE)

"Other people don't live like this; they can't!" is an exclamation often heard in our van or home whenever Alison and I are hit with a case of *kidstration*. The word is derived from the English words "kid" meaning "child or young person" and "frustration" meaning "irritated or fed up." Kidstration attacks are often unpredictable and can happen at any time to any parent. (If you know parents who say they don't experience this, they are lying.) It happens far too often for us.

I'll be honest; there are times I just lose it. I do. Like when the kids are fighting in the back of the van. I usually build from a mild "Let's all just quiet down now," to a hit-the-brakes, jerk-my-head-around, red-faced, "THE NEXT PERSON THAT SAYS A WORD, I'M TALKIN' ONE LITTLE WORD, IS GONNA GET THE HARD-EST WHOOPIN' YOU EVER HAD!"

Now the end does not always justify the means, but let me tell you, folks, this method works.

Now please don't send me letters on the dangers of

corporal punishment because you're not going to change my mind. I love my children dearly and would never, ever do anything to hurt them physically, emotionally, or any other way. However, my parents were raised getting "whoopin's" on their rumps, I got whoopin's on my rump, and my kids—if they openly and defiantly disobey my instructions—will themselves get whoopin's on their rumps. These are very rare as the mere threat usually creates an entirely different attitude in the back of the van.

Now, our household is made up of Dad, Mom, and three kids. We are a Christian family. We go to church, we pray, we read the Bible and Bible stories, and we talk openly about God and Jesus Christ. We talk often about loving one another and others.

At the same time, we may appear to be a pagan family. We argue, we raise our voices, we make faces, and we say things to provoke one another—none of which are spiritual gifts, as far as I can determine. Some among us even pull hair, wrestle, bite, and exhibit other forms of less than exemplary behavior.

We are a self-professed family of hypocrites.

Why is this? I often wonder. Now, let me say while Alison and I do argue from time to time (and I forgive her every time—that's just the kind of guy I am), we don't wrestle with—or bite—each other. She says I make faces, but I deny that charge. The bottom line is that—while less than perfect—we do love each other and demonstrate that love to the kids. But what is it that makes the kids misbehave, disobey, and generally cause their parents to yell and turn red in the face?

The other day we were eating at Danver's, a roast beef and hamburger place in my hometown of Tupelo, and Wesley started telling me how Wriley had started a fight the night before at their grandparents' house. She did this and she did that, which caused him to do this and to do that. And on and on and on we go. I've heard this story a thousand times. It's never his fault.

By the way, when was the last time you heard a six-year-old at the dinner table say something like: "Mom and Dad, I want to say I'm sorry right here in front of the entire family. It was my anger, it was my mouth, and it was my fist that caused the problem with my elder sister. I am taking full responsibility for my own actions and am prepared to take—like the man I am—the necessary discipline which you alone can determine is just, fair, and for my long-term societal well-being." A simple unsolicited "Um, I'm sorry" would be refreshing.

The heart and soul of the Christian faith is love of God first, and from that flows a love for our fellowman (including our brothers and sisters). Our love is demonstrated by how we treat one another. "Do unto others as you would have them do unto you," is the Golden Rule of yesterday, today, tomorrow, and forever.

One of the main responsibilities God gives parents is to bridle the passions of their children. The Scripture says to "train up" a child in the fear and admonition of the Lord. The values that flow from love should be charity, kindness, gentleness, respect, and reverence, among others. All of these lead to civility which in turn leads to a healthy society.

To a certain extent, kids will be kids, I suppose. For as long as there are minivans and station wagons, there will be cries of "Mama, he's on my side of the line." But at some point children must grow out of childish ways. They must learn to bridle their passions, love God and one another, and live out that love.

It's the same way with adults who follow Christ. We must die to self and take up our cross and follow Him. Daily. Love our neighbor as ourselves. We need God to train us in His ways and we must be willing to yield to that training.

There's a lot of yelling, screaming, and fighting in the world today. We live in a very violent and, in many ways, barbaric society. And I don't want to sound smug or trite here. But we who call the name above all names —the name of Jesus Christ—had better learn to live out our message of love and hope before the world around us, or things are going to get a whole lot more barbaric in these United States of America.

The only hope for America, the only hope for the world, is Jesus Christ.

Two Things to Remember

1. Jesus said we are to love one another in word and deed.
2. Other than the few problems I've mentioned above, my children are nearly perfect. How about yours?

THIS IS NOT HAPPENING TO ME

Things don't always go as planned, do they? Oftentimes problematic situations and circumstances just pop up out of nowhere. You can make all the budgets you want and then your back goes out, which means x-rays, which means $1,000. Or someone rams your car in the rear, so you'd like to put the trunk back where it was meant to be, but the individual who smashed your trunk doesn't have insurance. This kind of thing happens every day to hardworking Americans like you and me. It's not fair, but does your insurance company care about that? Noooooooooooo.

Yes, the unexpected, the surprises, are just an everyday part of life. You can prepare and plan all you want, then look up into a beautiful clear blue sky, feeling no pain, ready to praise the Lord, and then SPLAT!—there's bird splat on your forehead. Life is just like that. Honestly. The Bible warns that life can be this way. God controls all; we control very little. Dr. James Dobson says, "If you think you don't have any problems today, just wait until tomorrow." How true.

Now, I'm not the world's best planner. My wife, Alison, would be among the five most organized people in the world if a contest was held, but I'm rather average on this front. The upside of not being so organized is that surprises don't tend to bother me as much as they do people like Alison. But a couple of years back, I experienced one of the worst "surprises" of my life.

I was in the Dallas–Fort Worth airport on this particular day, waiting to board my flight to Lubbock, Texas. I figured it up the other day—while in DFW— I've now spent approximately one-tenth of my life in the DFW airport. Another 10 percent has been spent in the Atlanta airport. This is a major reason I struggle with daily devotions. Several times I have actually flown over my own house twice trying to get home. Seriously, if you fly from Dallas to Atlanta you go right over Tupelo, Mississippi. I usually look out the window and point down to my house to the folks next to me. Most of the time, they're unimpressed. Then if you fly from Atlanta to Memphis like I have to do, you go right over Tupelo, Mississippi. Again. It's frustrating. I've thought about buying me a good parachute.

But while sitting in the DFW airport on this one occasion studying people—and there are some strange people walking among us, if you haven't noticed—I drank a large bottle of water. I still can't believe I'm paying for water today. To me it's like paying for air to breathe. It was hot and I was thirsty. A few minutes later, those flying to Lubbock were told to board the shuttle bus that would take us out to our plane, which held about fifty people.

I can't say much to our three young kids when they want to stop five times on a two-hour trip to take a restroom break because I usually go right along with them. I drink a lot of liquids. While on the shuttle bus, I got that old familiar feeling. You know the one. That uncomfortable feeling common to man. It wouldn't be very long until the water would complete its own short trip and I would need to visit the restroom. *I'll go when I get on the plane,* I thought to myself. *No problem.*

When I got seated on the plane the feeling grew stronger. I looked back down the aisle but the traffic was too heavy, so I would just wait a little longer. Or so I thought.

When we got into the air, I was getting very uncomfortable when the flight attendant came over the public address and made all the normal announcements and I heard her say something about the "lavatory." However, someone was talking beside me and I didn't quite make out what she had said. I was starting to get uncomfortable. Real uncomfortable. A few minutes later the flight attendant walked by.

"Can I use the restroom now?" I asked, knowing that the seat belt sign was still on.

"I'm sorry, sir, did you not hear my announcement? The lavatory is inoperable," she said.

"I'm sorry? What do you mean?" Her words were

not registering with my mind, or body, which was in denial.

"You can't use the lavatory, sir. It doesn't work."

I was stunned. In total disbelief.

"You're kidding me, right?"

"No sir. I am sorry. Can I help you with anything else?"

"No, not really," I responded, trying to be as polite as possible. "Ma'am, let me get this straight. You mean to tell me there are fifty people on here for a one-hour-and-fifteen-minute flight and the bathroom doesn't work?"

"That's right, sir, I'm sorry."

"Isn't this against FCC regulations or something?"

"You mean the FAA, sir."

"Yeah, that too. In fact, ma'am, I think this violates the policy of a whole lot of other three-letter agencies including the FBI, CIA, NFL, NBA, CBS, NBC, and the NRA. And we don't even want to think about what will happen if the NCAA finds out about this."

People were staring at me. I wasn't being very charitable, to say the least. But I didn't care. Put yourself in my shoes.

Normally I'm sort of an easy-come, easy-go type of guy. It takes a lot to get me upset. But this—this was serious.

Now I'm not one for breaking rules, but I was at the point of not caring. *I'll go anyway when she's not looking,* I thought to myself. *This is one rule I'm breaking. And if*

I get caught, well, I'll deal with the consequences afterward.

Like Father Time, Mother Nature doesn't wait.

Well, she went on down the aisle and I quickly surveyed the situation. Man, I was hurting. We've all been there a time or two, haven't we? If I were the suing type, I could have won a lawsuit against the airline in a trial. Any judge and jury would have sympathized with me.

Evidently, I wasn't alone. The next thing I know, the guy right behind me, in dire straits himself, decides to make a break for it. He quickly moved out of his seat and slid down the aisle to the lavatory door, almost in one motion, trying to avoid the eagle-eyed flight attendant.

But just as he was about to open the door, here she came saying both politely and forcefully, "Sir! Sir! You can't go in there."

I didn't hear what he said in return. He was somewhat embarrassed, I'm sure, as anyone would be.

Oh no, I thought. *She sat this poor guy down and now she's guarding the door. This is it for me.* I felt like a trapped rabbit unable to free myself. Then the idea came to me. Necessity, as they say, is the mother of invention.

Sitting beside me was a man reading a magazine. We had not said anything to each other to that point. I wasn't much in the mood for talking, for obvious reasons, but I had to try something. I looked at my watch. Fifty minutes until we land in Lubbock. *This is not happening to me,* I thought. The idea: Start up a conversation with the man sitting beside me in hopes it would take my mind off my most serious predicament. This was my only chance. So I sat as still as I could, turned to the gentleman sitting next to me and just blurted out, "So, where you from?" *Please talk to me, mister,* I thought.

"Omaha," he said in friendly tone, looking up from his magazine and then back down.

Thank You, Lord. The last thing I needed at this point was to be shocked with rudeness.

"Oh yeah, what part of Omaha?"

Like I knew. I've never been to Omaha in my life. I wouldn't know one part of town from another. So he told me which community he lived in and described a few landmarks. I shook my head "yes," as if I knew where he was talking about.

"So what do you do for a living?" was my obvious next question.

"I'm a rep for a chemical company. Herbicides, pesticides, that sort of thing. For farmers."

"Oh yeah? We do a lot of farming where I'm from," I said.

"Where you from?" he said.

Yes, he was taking the bait.

"Mississippi," I said, my voice changing from a high pitch to normal to higher pitched.

"We do some business in Mississippi. What town?"

Well, we went on talking about everything from the Nebraska Cornhuskers to the best ribs restaurant in Memphis. And it worked. The occupation of my mind put by body in neutral for those fifty minutes. We did, however, experience some severe turbulence just a few minutes out of Lubbock, which made things worse. But we landed, and I made it. And I passed on the "beverage of your choice" during the flight.

Like I said in the introduction, I've had some real half-baked experiences in my life.

I don't know about you, but the things that really test me in this life are the unexpected. Those things you can't plan for, foresee, or predict. We all like surprises of the pleasant variety. It's the bad news that we have a hard time dealing with, oftentimes. Our child brings home failing grades. We find out our best friend is leaving his family and getting a divorce. We lose our job. We find out that a family member has cancer. When we receive negative news from life, the test comes in how we react. Do we go into a shell? Do we lash out in anger? Do we get mad at God? Or do we do the very best we can to fight through the difficult, the ugly, and the disappointing, keeping our faith in the Lord to be with us through it all?

The best way to prepare for the unexpected is to be grounded in God's Word, to pray daily and often, to develop strong relationships with other believers, and hold on to God's promises that He will be with us through the ups and downs of life. Remember, God is there. God does care.

Two Things to Remember

1. Each one of us will have trials and tests in our spiritual lives. And oftentimes these trials and tests come as a result of something we could not have seen coming. The unexpected. We can take comfort in knowing Jesus said He will never leave us or forsake us whatever life throws our way.
2. I don't drink bottled water before getting on airplanes anymore. You just never know.

SQUATTING AND SQUANDERING

"Church May Force Out Squatter," read the headline datelined Akron, Ohio, a couple of years back. I know you're wondering what a "squatter" is. I'll explain in a minute.

As I understand Christianity from reading the Bible, it is an active faith. Jesus told His followers to go and spread His message to the ends of the Earth. He told them to be salt and light in the culture and environment in which they lived. Faith without works is dead, says the book of James.

That is why I have a hard time understanding Christian separatist movements. I can understand separating oneself from the world for a season perhaps, but not a lifetime. How can you influence the world around you if you never mix around in it a little?

Jim Dunn said he was doing "God's will." Jim's the above-mentioned squatter in Akron. Allow me to quote from the Associated Press: "Jim Dunn believes God told him to go live outside First Congregational Church, so he set up a makeshift tent on the front yard.

"That was thirteen months ago. At first he was welcome, but his lengthy stay and the arrival of a few rats have made church members reconsider their generosity.

"Asking God for guidance, they will vote at their annual meeting on whether to oust him from church property.

"Dunn has spent his days sitting on an overturned bucket under a tree outside the church since April 1995, when Springfield Baptist Church asked him to leave its property. His only companion is a nine-year-old collie, Kay, who ignores the occasional six-inch rat scurrying nearby.

'I'm not living my will, I'm living God's will,' said Dunn, fifty-three.

"He has no visible means of support and won't divulge his past. The *Akron Beacon Journal* quoted relatives as saying the family was aware of his living conditions but would not discuss his background.

" 'People have tried to help him,' a sister told the newspaper. 'This is his choice.' "

The article went on, "He was never a member of First Congregational and doesn't attend its services. He was, however, a member for several years of Springfield Baptist. He won't go to a shelter two blocks away from First Congregational. He doesn't shower, but uses restrooms in nearby service stations."

Now—like it or not—you know what a squatter is. Even Mr. Bojangles sang and danced, Jim. You just sit.

What do you think about people like Jim? Many

people would have pity for him. I don't mean this to sound harsh, but I don't feel sorry for people like Jim. What's there to feel sorry for him about? This is the lifestyle he's chosen. After talking with many ministers and others who have dealt with the homeless, I have been shocked to learn that a high percentage of these people have little or no desire to improve their situation. At least if it means working for money or having to be personally responsible for themselves. Many have become addicted to the handouts and answering to no one.

But you know, the only real difference between Jim and many folks in the pews Sunday after Sunday is that most people bathe, hold a job, and sit *inside* the church building. Other than that, a lot of us are just like the very misguided Jim Dunn. We're just "go-through-the-Sunday-morning-motions" Christians.

But Jesus calls us to be something quite the opposite. He's called us to be about His Father's business using the gifts and talents He's blessed us with. He's called us to live out our faith in order that those around us—who don't know the Lord—might see our good works and glorify our Father in heaven.

I think of a song I learned as a kid at Vatican Bible School. Yes, even as a young Protestant boy from Mississippi my mom and dad would save their pennies to send me across the Atlantic ocean every summer to Rome where I would play ring-around-the-rosy and do arts and crafts with the pope. I remember the pope, a nice man, was constantly tripping on his robe when we played red-rover and would often yell out something in Polish that I could never. . . Wait a minute! Did I say Vatican? What is wrong with me? Would you just slap me, please? What I meant to say was VACATION Bible School. There is a big difference. I don't even know if the pope holds VBS at the Vatican. Anyway, it was here—at VBS at our little Methodist church—I learned this song: "This little light of mine, I'm gonna let it shine. This little light of mine, I'm gonna let it shine, let it shine, let it shine, let it shine. Hide it under a bushel—NO, I'm gonna let it shine. Hide it under a bushel—NO, I'm gonna let it shine, let it shine, let it shine, let it shine." So, I'm a little off-key. You get the idea.

Now, I'm going to make a judgmental statement here. I know this is risky in this day and age of political correctness and everybody blaming everybody else for their problems. But my man Jim is no more doing the will of God by sitting around all day every day on a bucket watching the grass grow and the paint dry, than is the man in the moon. In fact, the man in the moon is probably more nearly doing the will of God than Jim.

Jim could do something with his life, but, sadly, he's unwilling. How often are we like this in our response to God's calling?

Well, the church did vote to evict Jim from its property. He wound up in prison because he went back to the property after being forced to leave.

I liked church member Arthur Wallach's answer for Jim. Wallach told Jim he should follow the itinerant preaching style of Jesus: "It's time for him to travel and take the Gospel message somewhere else."

The same can be said for many of us who squat inside the church.

Two Things to Remember

1. James 2:17 says: "Thus also faith by itself, if it does not have works, is dead" (NKJV).
2. Fortunately, the Squatters denomination is having a hard time finding converts. Perhaps it's because the sanctified sitting cuts down on home visitations.

Q. Who Really Started the Fight, Cain or Able?

Richard B. Tyson from Oak Toad, New Mexico

A. Thanks, Richard, and may I say, this is one slightly better than average question. All Oak Toadians should be proud of you. And I know they are.

Now to your question about Cain and Able. In the first place Richard, it's Abel, not Able, so next time you write please speel the names correctly.

The Bible, of course, records that Cain was the one who let his emotions get the best of him and killed Abel. Genesis 4:8 states that Cain, "talked with Abel his brother; and it came to pass, when they were in the field, that Cain rose up against Abel his brother and killed him" (NKJV).

Reviewing here, Cain "talked," "rose up," and "killed." I say the ol' boy had a bit of short fuse.

In fact, Abel probably was stunned by this sudden turn of events.

"Why, Cain, brother, you just talked and rose. Now must you slay me?"

"Indeed I must, Abel. There's only just so much talking and rosing a man can do before he must kill."

"Art thou still upset because thy brother beat you in Monopoly for the sixteenth straight time last night?"

Unfortunately, Abel never got an answer.

Yes, Cain was the guilty party and started the fight. That is the short answer to your question, Richard. However, some liberal theologians argue that there are two sides to this story and that Abel actually may have taunted Cain with redneck jokes.

Cain, after all, was a "tiller of the ground." Abel, on the other hand, was a slick, Harvard-educated "keeper of the sheep." Abel fancied himself a refined individual and often wore fig leafs purchased at Niemann Marcus, although refined was a relative term in those days since there wasn't exactly a neighborhood "on the other side of the tracks" with people to compare one's refined self to. In fact, in those days, there weren't any tracks at all. (Later the American Track Society would form, but this was several thousands of years after Cain and Abel and basically included only those who had won Gold medals such as Jesse Owens and Carl Lewis.)

"If it takes a rake to clean your fingernails, you might be a redneck!" Abel would say laughingly, according to some liberal theologians. Of course, Abel would add insult to injury by laughing out loud at his own redneck jokes as the crowds were slim at this point in history.

This constant mockery really ticked Cain off and

so he tried talking with his brother.

"Let me tell you something, you little jerk," Cain said. "If it wadn't for me, you and your type wouldn't eat!"

"What does 'wadn't' mean?" Abel would say with a smug smirk. "And what do you mean 'me and my type'? There's only one of me and one of you, you ignorant redneck. You make me laugh. HA!"

That, according to the theory these liberal theologians support, is all it took for Cain—not being familiar with the "turn the other cheek" commandment—to shut his brother up once and for all. There were to be no more redneck jokes until a fortyish IBM computer analyst from Atlanta, Georgia, named Jeff Foxworthy came along in the mid-1990s A.D.

Ironically, Foxworthy made a killing telling redneck jokes. Soon history books will include the name Jeff Foxworthy for future generations as an example of how one individual with one line of jokes—which he milked until the udder was blistered dry—could rake home a small fortune and never, ever have to return to IBM again. This, my friends, is what America is all about. Opportunity.

That, Richard, should give you some historical context for the answer to your question.

Thanks for writing, and Oak Toad should be proud of you for asking the question that many wanted to ask but were afraid it might be a stupid question.

GIFT-GIVING MISGIVINGS

Gift giving is great, isn't it? The Bible says it is better to give than to receive. Most of us do get a special feeling when we give someone a gift we know they will love. Birthdays, special occasions, and especially Christmas, are days Americans love to give gifts to one another. And we love receiving them as well.

But did you know that according to a survey by the American Express Travel Related Services Company, one in four of us has actually passed on a gift given to us to someone else? It's true. The American Express Travel Related Services people wouldn't lie about something as important as this!

All I have to say is, for shame! You people kill me! I would never, ever. . . Okay, okay, my hand's up too. But it's been a while. Last Christmas, I think it was.

If gift giving is a great American tradition, I guess passing on a gift someone gave us is a great American tradition as well. Now keep in mind this one-in-four number represents people who actually admitted to doing this. And this is one of those questions that even the people who answer "yes," and are honest, still tuck their heads when admitting to it.

Let's see, it's an ugly sweater your aunt gave you and so you—being the thoughtful type—decide to give it to your brother next Christmas. But what if your aunt who gave you the ugly sweater is there when he opens the box? What then? Answer. Tell her you loved the sweater so much that you went out and bought your brother one just like it.

Yes, technically you are lying. Technically.

Now if she starts looking at the tag real close and sees you got the sweater last year for the same discounted price she got it for, and at the same store, then you've got problems.

"Why, if it ain't the same price and store, Aunt Josie, I'll be John Brown. What are the chances of that happening?"

How about that Christmas fruitcake? We've got one in our family that's been passed around for seven years now. Everybody knows it, but no one says anything. It's been in my freezer twice for one year each time. That fruitcake's been in four different states and three time zones. I thought about throwing it away, but I want to see who the brave soul is that actually eats it. Besides, it's kind of a Christmas tradition now.

What are those green things anyway? Are they from the fruit family? I don't think so. I've been to the grocery store many times in my life and not once have I seen these green things among the other fruits such as bananas, apples, and oranges. I've only seen them in fruitcakes at Christmastime, which leads me to believe they aren't fruit at all but are actually unused automotive parts melted down and mixed in with cake mix in hopes that no one will notice. Well, I did. And I, for one, have a rule against eating melted-down automotive parts. And if I'm the only one who believes this, then so be it.

Now we know, again, thanks to the fine folks at the American Express Travel Related Services who wouldn't lie about such things, that 25 percent of us pass on gifts we don't want to others as gifts. But how about the flip side of that? You know, buying some member of your immediate family a gift they have no practical use for, just so that you can use it.

I've got a confession to make here. When I was nine, I did this. Mom gave me a few dollars to buy my little one-year-old brother Mark a gift. So I bought him an electric football game. Man, I had a ball with that thing. I wore it out before he was old enough to use it, though. I did let him bang on it a few times just to ease my conscience, and I pretended it was a wet field when he would drool. Sorry, I have to break this to you in a book, bro. Hey, I was told it was the thought that counts anyway.

Speaking of thoughts that count, it was our Heavenly Father who was thinking of you and me when He gave us the greatest give of all, His Son Jesus Christ. The Bible says in the gospel of John 3:16, that, "God so loved the world that He gave His only begotten Son, that whoever believes in Him should not perish but have everlasting life" (NKJV).

If we only receive God's free gift of Jesus into our hearts, the Bible promises we will live forever. Simply put, that means when we die we go to heaven to be with Jesus and all those who've gone before us who also trusted in Him.

And the wonderful thing about the gift of Jesus is that we can, indeed, pass it on to others while maintaining His presence for ourselves. In fact, that's what God wants us to do.

And for what it's worth, there are no green things.

TWO THINGS TO REMEMBER

1. God offers us the free gift of eternal life if
    only we will receive His Son Jesus Christ
    into our hearts.
2. If you have information that reveals to
    Americans what those green things in
    fruitcakes are, please contact me. I have
    taken this up as a personal crusade. Move
    over, Ralph Nader.

TOM AND JERRY

I was fired up and ready. For the third time in my life I was going deep-sea fishing. And this time, I was going to catch the Big Fish.

The first time I ventured out to sea was on a family vacation in 1979 in Ft. Walton Beach, Florida. Dad paid $150 to take Mom, my two sisters, my brother, and me out in the Gulf of Mexico. Within an hour some dark clouds came up, the waters got very rough, and one by one we all got sick to the point of leaning over the boat and doing what people do when they get seasick and lean over the boat. (I would say "throw up" but I don't like using such a disgustingly descriptive phrase in my writing because people turn you off when you introduce "throw up" into a story. Besides, it's unnecessary when you have alternatives like "upchuck" or "puke.")

The second experience for me was during family vacation in 1997 on Hilton Head Island, South Carolina. My father-in-law, Jim, paid for my son Wesley and me to go out on a boat called the Captain Hook.

It was a six-hour trip. Two hours out to sea, two hours with our hooks in the water, and two hours back. Looking back, I would say we got ripped off. We caught a few small fish, but nothing big. Nothing to brag about, like we had hoped for, but we had fun.

A few months later Alison and I had reason to be back on the South Carolina coast in charming and historic Charleston—or "Chalston" as some Southerners are prone to say—for a conference. A friend of mine, Nick Stavarz, invited me, and whoever I wanted to bring along, to go fishing on a chartered boat for a day in the Atlantic Ocean. This was to be a twelve-hour trip way out into *The Gulf Stream*. The Gulf Stream—of course—is where the Big Fish swim around looking for smaller fish to eat while they themselves try to keep from being eaten by even Bigger Fish. If you're a fish in the Gulf Stream, you're always watching your tail. Which, in large part, explains why a lot of fish spend the majority of their lives swimming in circles, never getting to experience the vast expanses of the seven seas. It also explains why so many fish have to be treated for dizziness when caught by marine biologists who study the behavioral habits of paranoid fish who are constantly watching their tails, the theme from *Jaws* continuously playing in their heads. Take it from someone who's never been a marine biologist, these fish have absolutely NO quality of life. Many wish they could be eaten and just get it over with.

Anyway, I knew my good friend Tom Minnery

was going to be at this same conference so I called him up and asked him to come along with us. He readily accepted.

The plan was for Tom and I to meet in the hotel lobby at five A.M. to catch a taxi down to the marina, about a fifteen-minute drive from our hotel. We would rendezvous with Nick there. Well, I got my wake up call at 4:30—which Alison really appreciated—and hopped in the shower, causing me to slip and almost bust my tail. Humans, when hopping on wet floors, are always having to watch their tails. I have since quit hopping around on wet floors at 4:30 in the morning and gone back to walking and stepping. But when I get really excited—as was the case here—I have been known to just start hopping out of control like a kangaroo. My family can't stand it when this happens in public.

I was downstairs by five. As I walked into the lobby, I looked out the door and saw our cab driver get out of his car and walk inside. He was a black fellow of medium height, stocky build, and looked about forty years old. He had on a T-shirt with a Bible on the front and the wording said "Need answers? Read the Bible," or something to that effect. The reason I can't remember exactly what it said is due to my handicap. I don't talk about it much, but when it's five o'clock in the morning I only have use of one eye and this one eye—it doesn't focus properly until 6:30. Around seven though—about the time my heart starts beating—the eyes begin to come to life and adjust themselves (all the while complaining and threatening to shut down again until about 8:30). Truth be known, I need drugs. But I'm afraid I'll get addicted.

Tom and I double-checked to make sure we had what we needed. We exchanged pleasantries with the cabbie as he walked over to the desk clerk—they obviously knew each other—and then poured himself a cup of hot coffee. Tom already had his in hand. Then we all went outside, climbed in the cab, and began driving away as I told the driver where we needed to go.

"I like your T-shirt," I said to him. (Tip: This is a great icebreaker with men. With women try: How'd you get those bags under your eyes?)

"Thanks," he responded.

"I'm Tim and this is Tom."

"I'm Jerry. Nice to meet you."

Taking off on the T-shirt, I asked Jerry a question.

"Do you always dress this tacky, Jerry? You look like a bum."

No, no, that's not what I asked. I'm not that tacky. What I said was "Are you a Christian?"

I fully expected a hearty, "Yes!" back at me. After all, he had a straightforward T-shirt advocating the Bible. But Jerry thought about it for a few seconds.

"Well, I guess you could say I'm a spiritual man."

"A spiritual man?"

"Yeah, I believe in treating others like I want to be treated, living a clean life, being responsible. You know, all those things."

Jerry's answer kind of threw me for a second. It sounded like a classic example of someone believing in good works or clean living as a means of salvation. But before I could gather my thoughts for a response (it usually takes me ten to fifteen minutes this early in the morning, which, as you can imagine, really hurts the continuity of a conversation), Tom—sharp as a tack—leaned forward and asked Jerry this question.

"If you were to die right here and now—would you go to heaven OR would you burn in hell for eternity?"

Way to go Tom, I thought. *I'm trying to build a rapport with this guy and you whip out the "burn in hell" question first thing in the morning. You're the man, Tom.*

"Heaven, I hope," responded Jerry.

"Based on what you just said, can I ask you a question?"

"Sure," responded Jerry.

"If you were standing at the pearly gates of heaven and St. Peter asked you why he should let you in, what would you say?"

"I'd say, 'look at my life.' "

Jerry then went on to share with Tom and I the fact that he was once—about five years before—addicted to drugs and alcohol. It had ruined his marriage and almost led to suicide. Then he began to credit God for saving him from total destruction and setting his life straight. Jerry even quoted some Bible verses.

"That's wonderful," Tom responded. "But you

know what? The Bible you're quoting says that none of us are clean enough or have done enough good works to make it into heaven. Those things—while admirable—are as filthy rags in the eyes of the Lord. We can't get into heaven with our works but rather our trust in Jesus Christ."

Jerry was shaking his head in agreement.

"Well, I believe that," he said.

I wondered if Jerry really meant it, or if he was just going along with Tom because he didn't want to be disagreeable. I know how this is, especially so early in the morning. Jerry could have said to me, "Just yesterday I drove this taxicab into outer space and had lunch with the Man in the Moon." And I would have said, "I believe that." Why argue with someone when you're having a hard time keeping your eyes open and the drool in your mouth, is the way I look at it.

Tom, Jerry, and I went on to have a good conversation. Jerry talked about how his grandmother had taken him to church as a child and how the lessons learned there had come back to him in his time of need. Tom commented on what a great lady Jerry's grandmother must have been to be such a loving, caring Christian example for him. It was a tender moment for us. Jerry's eyes looked like they were moistening. I then commented on an episode of *Seinfeld* I had seen recently and asked Jerry if he saw it. Immediately, there was stone silence in the car. Tom turned and gave me this blank stare as if I had ruined everything.

"What?" I said, looking back at him and then looking at Jerry's eyes in the rearview mirror. "What did I say wrong?"

"Nothing. We'll talk about it later," said Tom as he turned and stared out the window.

Actually, by the time we had arrived at the marina, Jerry had convinced Tom and I that he was indeed a Christian. We paid him and said so long.

Since it was still dark, Tom and I wandered around the marina for about half an hour before meeting a character named Bill who was to be our captain that day. Bill informed us there was a small boat advisory out and—unfortunately—he couldn't take us fishing. Our shoulders dropped. Tom took a swing at Bill, but missed. I looked down and spit on his shoes. All the anticipation and expectation shattered by mere eight-foot seas. *What a wimp this guy Bill is,* I thought. *Eight-foot seas! I've had eight-foot seas caused by cabin cruisers many times on the Tennessee-Tombigbee Waterway and it never stopped me.* But Barnacle Bill, who I'll save for another story, said to call him up another time and he'd be glad to take us fishing. But Tom lives in Colorado, I live in Mississippi, and Nick lives in Ohio. I don't think we'll be able to get together like this again. So why did the Lord let us get out of bed before daybreak only to have our hopes of catching THE BIG ONE dashed?

I think it was so Tom and Jerry could talk. And I know for me, it served as a reminder to take opportunities the Lord sends my way to share my faith in Him with others. And if it turns out they're already a member of the family, then praise the Lord for that as well!

By the way, did you see that episode of *Seinfeld* I was talking about? It was when. . .

Two Things to Remember

1. We need to take opportunities, when they present themselves, to share our faith in Jesus Christ with others. Jesus told us in Matthew 28:19: "Go therefore and make disciples of all the nations, baptizing them in the name of the Father and of the Son and of the Holy Spirit" (NKJV).
2. What a wimp this guy Bill was. If he can't handle eight-foot seas, he needs to get out of the business.

STARSTRUCK

If you would, I think it would be a good idea if you'd just sit down and take a deep breath before I tell you the news. Sitting down? Breathing deep? All right, then. Here goes. And I quote the October 27, 1997, edition of *USA Today*.

"WASHINGTON—Our own Milky Way galaxy is on a collision course with another galaxy but you won't need to buy that insurance just yet.

"The fireworks aren't due for more than 5 billion years—long after the sun has burned out and reduced Earth to a frigid cinder."

Take another deep breath. No, really, you need it. When I first read this I was at work and had to take the rest of the day off. Depressing news, it is. And just to think, I've been ironing all those years like it mattered.

Okay. Let's think rationally here. Try not to get too worked up. The one good thing about this problem is that we are not rushed to come up with answers. Now I wouldn't encourage procrastination, understand, because the years can fly by and like sands through the hourglass so are the days of our lives. Still, if NBC can milk a soap opera for thirty-five years or so and we can put a land rover on Mars, I think we can deal with this. Somehow, someway. With some 5 billion years—give or take a few million—to plan ahead, we should be able to figure out something, don't you think? But wait a minute; didn't I also just quote from the same story that before this cosmic collision, as if that's not enough to worry about, our own friendly sun will itself burn out? Yes, indeed, I did just quote from *USA Today* that before this cosmic collision, which I hate to keep bringing up, our own friendly and reliable Mr. Sunshine will, himself, give up the ghost.

What I want to know is why these scientists and *USA Today* decided to release this news just before the holidays? Why couldn't they at least wait until sometime in February when most Americans are already stuck inside their homes, good and depressed? But, no, these people decided to ruin the holiday season for all of us.

Now, it is a fact I graduated from Mississippi State University packing a four-year program into five (with a solid C+ average), and I have a better than average grasp of the sports world. So, after giving this matter a little thought—perhaps five minutes at the most—I have come to this conclusion. Although I have many skills and abilities, as you can clearly see, I am sorry to report that I will not be able to do anything about this impending calamity. (Note to the reader: "Impending" is used as a relative term in the previous sentence.) Again, I'm sorry. I know you were expecting more from me, as was my mama, but this is the hard truth that we all have to deal with.

Control. A lot of our attention in life is given to this matter of control. Control is like fire; it can have great benefits or it can be very destructive.

We are told in the Bible, for instance, that self-control is evidence of the Holy Spirit indwelling a Christian. This is also known sometimes as self-discipline. To the other extreme, some people have to be dominant in—or in control of—every situation. Most of the time these folks are known as "control freaks" because they always have to be in charge. Generally speaking, these individuals are unapproachable and unwilling to listen or give credence to anyone except themselves. I don't care to be around these people.

To me there are three levels of control in this life.
1. Self-control.
2. Circumstance-control.
3. No control.

The first, we are directly responsible to God for—responsible for our thoughts, actions, deeds, motivations, et cetera.

The second, we are somewhat responsible to God for. Are there steps we could take—or could have taken—that would change a circumstance or a situation? Would it be pleasing to the Lord that we do so? Of course, we must factor in other people's actions, but at the same time remember that God has no grand-children. In short, we are each individually responsible to God for at least our reaction to our circumstances.

The third level is where we have absolutely no control—like this galactic collision thing.

I know people—and you know them too—who spend the better part of their lives worrying about matters they can't control. How frustrating and point-less! Nothing positive can come from worrying about things we can't change or have absolutely no control over.

In the book of Daniel we find the story of three Hebrew men who were ordered by King Nebuchad-nezzar to fall down and worship a golden image that stood ninety-feet high which the king had ordered built. If they didn't, they were told they would be thrown into the nearby blazing furnace. Even at this point in history, blazing furnaces had the reputation of being very, very hot. Remember this story about Shadrach, Meshach, and Abednego? Sure, you do. These brave and faithful fellows—who served the one true God—looked the mighty King Nebuchadnezzar right in the eye and said, "Why do you, oh, king, have such a long and cumbersome name?" No, no, I'm sorry about that; actually, what they said was: "O Nebuchad-nezzar, we do not need to defend ourselves before you in this matter. If we are thrown into the blazing fur-nace, the God we serve is able to save us from it, and he will rescue us from your hand, O king. But even if he does not, we want you to know, O king, that we will not serve your gods or worship the image of gold you have set up" (Daniel 3:16–18 NIV).

This is a great biblical example of the kind of attitude we all should have. These guys realized they couldn't control what the king did with their bodies. However, they could control how they reacted to the situation at hand. And that's what they did. Likewise, it is our role to do all that we can for God, leaving the "worry" of everything else in this life in His trustworthy hands.

Now to be sure, a few million stars hurling across space in somewhat of an organized fashion can cause some serious damage and just might warrant a passing thought. So why don't you just go take sixty seconds or so and think about that. Never mind me, I'll just stand over here and stargaze for a minute. . . . Had enough? Okay. Now, walk over to the fridge and fix yourself a bologna sandwich just the way you like it. That, you can control.

Two Things to Remember

1. Concerning our control of—or lack of—the future, Jesus said in Matthew 6:34: "Therefore do not worry about tomorrow, for tomorrow will worry about its own things. Sufficient for the day is its own trouble" (NKJV).
2. Say, I'm kind of hungry. Do you want all of that sandwich?

Status Symbol

So there I was in the United States Capitol in Washington, D.C. I had just gotten off the elevator on the first floor and was looking for the men's room. I had already looked down two hallways to no avail. So when I exited the elevator, a little frustrated, I blurted out to the gentleman walking just a few feet in front of me, "Excuse me, sir, can you tell me where the men's room is?"

The sir turned around. *I know this face,* I thought to myself. *Yes, indeed. I've seen this face on CNN and C-SPAN.*

"Sure, it's just down that hall to the left," responded the face I knew from CNN and C-SPAN. He then pointed so that I would know exactly where he was talking about.

"I appreciate it," I responded.

The face was that of United States Senator William H. Frist of Tennessee. The arm that pointed also belonged to the senator.

Walking down the hall I had this thought. *Isn't that*

just like my life. Here I am in the most powerful city in the world, in the very building where national and international decisions of major importance are made every day. News made here goes around the world, and by chance I run into a United States senator in the hallway and what profound question do I pose? "Hey buddy, can you point me to a bathroom 'round here someplace?" Oh, that's good, Tim. Tell that one to your kid's civics class when you get home.

"Yeah, kids, as a matter of fact I did get to talk with a senator and the question I asked him was. . ."

My kids would never forgive me.

Then I started laughing. Yes, that is just like my life. But you know what? I don't really care. With rare exception, I am not impressed by the status symbols of this world. I don't mean that I am disrespectful of titles, offices, and such; I just mean that I'm not too moved by it all. Maybe I should be. I don't really know.

The same thing is true with me and clothing. I'm thirty-five years old and have never gone shopping for clothes for myself. Honestly. I hate dressing rooms. They're always cold; have you noticed? I'd rather be in prison. I also get a lot of hand-me-downs from my brother-in-law Neal Clement and a couple of other guys in my church. Alison takes care of the rest. This saves me money and keeps me from having to go to the mall with her and try on those stiff, scratchy new pants and shirts. And I couldn't tell you five name brands in the world of fashion.

One day when I came home from work Alison told

me she had a Tommy Hilfiger shirt for me to try on, to which I responded in all sincerity, "Who's he?" I knew that our minister of worship, Tommy Wilson, had given me some clothes he couldn't use any longer, but I didn't know this Hilfiger dude.

"Who's he?" Alison laughed. "You don't know the name Tommy Hilfiger? As in a famous-line-of-clothing Tommy Hilfiger?"

"Well, no; should I?"

"Here, just try the shirt on. You really should pay more attention to the world around you, Tim." Alison laughed some more.

I do remember asking my mama to buy me a couple of Izod shirts when I was in seventh grade. . .in 1975. All the popular kids at Milam Junior High School were wearing these shirts with the alligator on the pocket. So Mama bought me the alligator shirts. But I still didn't break into the popular crowd. I remember the first morning I wore one of my Izod shirts to school and all the popular kids were hanging out talking in kind of a circle—they were in the same place every day—before the bell rang to call us inside. Normally I hung out with some regular guys. But this particular morning I walked on by my regular buds, sporting my new status symbol on my chest. I was moving on up. I was going popular.

So I kind of milled around in the popular circle for a few minutes and got a few, "Who are you?" looks. I tried to talk to a couple of these popular people, but they would just give me one-word responses to my advances, always looking over my shoulder to see who else was around. I felt like saying, "Hey, look at me! I've got an alligator on my shirt, you idiot! I am popular! Respect it!" But I didn't. I just stood around for a few more minutes and then decided I didn't fit in. *These people are jerks*, I thought. So I went back to my regular friends. Thing about it was, my regular buds didn't say anything about my alligator shirt either. They just liked me because I was like them—regular—and because I knew more about sports then they did.

In Romans 2:11 the Bible says simply: "For God does not show favoritism" (NIV). Another way I've heard it put is that God is not a respecter of people. Meaning, He is not impressed with our last name, our bank account, our physical beauty, our degrees, or anything else used as measuring sticks by this world. The Lord looks on the heart.

My dad used to tell his four children that God cares as much about the ditchdigger as He does about the president of the United States. Isn't that good? And easily understood.

By the way, what ever happened to those alligator shirts anyway? Do popular people still wear them? And while we're on the subject, I wonder what ever happened to all those popular people. A lot of them still stand in circles, I'm told. Cocktail parties, I think they call them. And I still don't fit in.

Oh, well. The life of this regular guy goes on.

TWO THINGS TO REMEMBER

1. God doesn't show favoritism nor does He measure us by worldly things. God's grace is available to all who will come to Him regardless of our worldly status.
2. Right now I am wearing an alligator shirt. What's that trash you've got on?

Q. Why Did Matthew Get to Go First Instead of Mark, Luke, or John?

Tang Simmons of DeLeon, Florida

A. I've often pondered this question myself, Tang, which obviously makes it a very intelligent inquiry. Well, the reason or reasons—it seems to me—had nothing to do with the first names of these writers, since each of them had the first name "Accordingtothegospelof." This was a very popular first name back when the New Testament was being written. Despite the fact that it caused the inkwells to all dry up and was very cumbersome to write on checks or on water tanks, a practice that many teenage pranksters pulled back then and still do today, as a matter of fact. Later the inkwells were converted to oil wells and Middle Easterners did quite well in that business.

Another possible reason we can forget about is the idea that the guys huddled up and decided to go in alphabetical order. If that were the case, Luke would have gone first followed by. . .wait a minute. . . A, B, C, D, (excuse the under-the-breath singing) J,

K, L, M. . . No, John would have gone first and, ironically, Matthew would have gone last.

What happened here, Tang, is—you know what, I think I will take a little editorial liberty at this point and change your name. From now on I will refer to you, Tang, as Sir Lancelot. It's much more distinguished and if there is a drink of the same name it would have to be a fine wine and not some powdered drink astronauts use on long trips to do whatever they do up there. Besides racking up incredible long-distance bills talking to Houston about stuff that they only pretend to understand in an attempt to impress—and in some cases intimidate—the rest of us who have difficulty keeping up with our car keys, much less operating a space shuttle.

Sorry there, Sir Lancelot, I got a little sidetracked. But it just kills me to see my tax dollars wasted almost as much as it does to see paper wasted on stories in books that add absolutely nothing to the betterment or intellectual development of man- or womankind but rather are silly drivel having no real meaning or purpose.

Now back to your question. I believe Matthew went before Mark, Luke, and John because he wrote the most chapters. It's simple, really; he outworked the other guys. Matthew put his nose to the grindstone, whatever that means, and penned twenty-eight chapters while Mark only got sixteen, Luke just twenty-four, and John a mere twenty-one. The grindstone caused much pain to Matthew's nose area and gave him severe migraine headaches, but it paid off for him and he took great pride in this accomplishment. Although the feeling was short-lived when he was told that pride was actually a sin.

After they each had completed their manuscripts, they were having coffee at the Acts of the Apostles Bed & Breakfast where the four often gathered to discuss the events of the day. John brought up the fact that Jesus said that in the kingdom of heaven the last would be first and the first would be last, which really bummed out Matthew and he consequently lost his appetite. In fact, he left early without eating another bite of his pancakes.

So there, Sir Lancelot, is your answer. Please write again and remember what Matthew always said: "If you ain't the lead dawg, the view's always the same."

The Cow Jumped Over the Moon, Almost

"Yeah, when pigs fly," is an old American expression. Translated this means, whatever you're talking about could never—or will never—actually happen because it would absolutely deny reality in the same way flying swine would deny reality. God won't allow it. Well, boys and girls, I've got a pig-flying story in a minute that you're not going to believe.

Trust. Honesty. Reputation. Credibility. All these words are important to our witness as Christians. If we lose our believability with other people, we do great damage to the cause of Christ. Obviously, we who follow Him know that when we fail, it is we who fail and not Christ, but still, in the eyes of others, we represent Jesus so, therefore, if we are dishonest it is a reflection on His name. Make sense?

One of the values my mama taught me as a child growing up on 1411 Van Buren Street was to always think the best of people. She also told me that I couldn't continue to grow up on the actual street and that at some point I would tire of dodging cars and need to come inside the actual house. As usual, Mom was right. When I was seven, that's what I did. But this idea of always thinking the best of people was more than a little naive, I've since learned. In fact, that ideal has gotten me used and abused on many occasions. Many lowlifes out there look at us good-hearted people as fools. Doormats. I hate to say it, but it's the truth. Yet, I still think it's probably the best way to look at the world, even if we must be taken advantage of by the jerks of this world from time to time.

Along these same lines, I've kind of adopted a philosophy of my own that I try to live by. That is: I try to trust people and give them the benefit of the doubt unless or until they give me reason not to. I try to apply this view even when a situation looks and feels like a case of my being lied to or cheated.

But there are times when honesty can almost seem counterproductive. The following story is a case in point. This news item (which I am in no way making up) first appeared in the July 1997 edition of *Flying*. This magazine calls itself the "World's Most Widely Read Aviation Magazine." And I quote: "The crew of a trawler which sank in the Sea of Japan claimed the ship went down after being struck by a cow which fell out of the clear blue sky and went straight through the hull. No one believed their tale until, a few weeks later, confirmation came from Russia that the crew of one of its military cargo jets had stolen a cow they found wandering on a Siberian airfield and loaded it aboard for the flight home. While the airplane was cruising at 30,000 feet the terrified, unrestrained beast ran amok," (I'll say), "so the crew lowered the cargo ramp and it jumped out." (Wrong day to pitch a cow fit.)

And these guys were worried about rough seas. Ha!

This is why I've always said—and I've been mocked by many for having such a "paranoid" view of ocean travel—that when you're out on the high seas you absolutely have to plan for everything. Well, where are the mockers now? I am here to tell you—as a veteran of two deep-sea fishing adventures and as someone who has watched many Royal Caribbean ads on television—hurricanes, whale tails, whirlpools, motion sickness, and the ever-increasing danger of cows falling from the sky are *all* potential fun-killers.

If I might, I would like to take a moment and re-create that fateful day in the fateful Sea of Japan and translate what was spoken in fateful Japanese as the fateful fishing crew witnessed and experienced this event. (This also can be found in Revelation chapter 76 as a sign that the *Lone Ranger* will soon return as a television series.) Imagine the captain of this boat, up on top, lying back, looking up in the sky with his hands behind his head and his feet crossed. Just relaxing for a few moments in the bright, warm sunshine.

Captain: "Hey, Jo Na, throw your net out and
come up here and have a seat, buddy."

Jo Na: "No problem, Captain."

Captain: "You know, Jo Na, I've been doing a lot of thinking lately."

Jo Na: "What about, Captain?"

Captain: "Next week I'm making my last payment after twenty years of busting my tail out here on the sea keeping this baby in tip-top condition. I checked the value a few weeks ago and you know what? I can actually retire with the profit I can make off this lady, Jo Na."

Jo Na: "No kidding, sir?"

Captain: "No kidding, Jo Na. I quit making my insurance payments last week and I've got a buyer. It's going to be a good life, Jo Na. Yes sir, a good life indeed."

Jo Na: "That's great, Captain. What about me?"

Captain: "Well, Jo Na, I've been giving that some thought and—say, what's that black-and-white dot falling from the sky?"

And what about this captain's SOS message? Again, Japanese translated to English.

Captain: "No, you idiot, I didn't say holy cow! I said we've got a hole in the boat from a cow that fell from the sky and busted through our hull! We need help now!"

SOS man: "Yeah, Captain, and I'm Santa

Claus. Say, if one of my runaway reindeer happens to land on your boat, you call me back now, you hear?"

Well, no one believed these guys when they testified that a cow had fallen from the sky and sunk their boat. But when all the information was brought to light, these guys were found to be telling the truth.

On a related matter, we need to be careful about judging people when we don't know all the facts about a particular situation. Oh, how we love to do this. We make rash statements and criticize others when we haven't walked a mile in their shoes or only know half the story.

There have been times when I've had to discipline my children in public. To the casual observer this can be a spectacle. There have been times that I'm sure I've looked like a very harsh and mean parent because I've raised my voice or put my finger in one of my children's chests to really get their attention. However, what the public didn't see was how my child had been disobedient and talking back for the thirty minutes prior to my emotional exhibition of parenting splendor. Context helps our understanding and our ability to relate or have compassion.

Finally, honesty is still the best policy. Even if it would be more convenient to be dishonest or stretch the truth a little.

Now, please allow me to talk to you about your

future. I've just gotten into the insurance business, you know. And this new policy will protect you and your loved ones in the event a cow should fall from the sky and smash through your roof. Oh, and don't think it can't happen. I beg you, for the sake of your children, please, you need this protection. You'll sleep easier at night knowing that if a cow did come crashing through your bedroom ceiling and killed you dead, your loved ones would be taken care of. What do you say? Just give me your bank account number and sign right here and you'll never have to think about this potential horror again. Trust me.

Two Things to Remember

1. Although some say it naive, we need to be willing to give people the benefit of the doubt on questions of honesty and truthfulness unless, or until, they prove that trust unmerited. "Try to think the best of people," is the advice my mama gave me.
2. No word on what the cow's last moos were as it fell from the plane.

LOVE AND MARRIAGE

When I travel I do a lot of scanning on the radio. Just like TV-channel flipping—or surfing, I suppose it's called in 1999—men also do this with the radio. I scan until I find a talk show I'm interested in or a song I like. Then I listen a while, sing out loud most of the time, and then scan some more. One evening, recently, I was cutting across Alabama coming home from a trip to Atlanta and my scan came across an advertisement promoting an on-line matchmaking service. "Find the man or woman that fits the qualities you're looking for on the Internet," said the soothing voice. My thought: "Some people are really desperate." Shopping for a mate like you would shop for a used boat? I don't know what to think about these kinds of services. Seems kind of cold and sterile to me. But then, I've never had to look, hope, and pray for the right woman, either. I've already married her. In fact, if you will excuse the self-indulgence, Alison and I celebrated our fifteenth anniversary July 28, 1999.

It was another hot and humid Mississippi Saturday

afternoon in 1984. We were married at the Good News Church in Tupelo by Pastor Billy Funderburk. This was just before the video craze hit America, so all we have are photographs. I like still pictures better anyway. They give you a chance to look, reflect, and remember without having to constantly rewind.

Speaking of pictures, have you ever noticed how you let someone look at your family photos and they run through like sixty of them in a minute and a half? Americans, we don't care about other people's pictures. Oh, sure, we may ask an insincere question or two as we flip through but, really, they mean nothing to us, let's be honest. Well, this is a practice I think needs to stop. And to this end I vow here and now—before all of you readers—to do everything one humor writer can do to make people care—really care—about my family pictures. I hope you'll do the same. Together, we can bring about change.

The week before the wedding, Mom bought me some new pants and a jacket to wear as we exited the church under heavy rice fire. One of the photos we have in our wedding book is of me in the driver's seat closing the door to my orange 1977 Buick Le-Sabre as we're about to leave the parking lot to go on the honeymoon. My arm is propped up on the steering wheel and featured prominently on the jacket sleeve is a big ol' price tag. Kind of like Minnie Pearl. And I'm just smiling real big for the camera. I was cool. We laugh every time we pull that photo out.

Mama has another picture in her photo album, this one from my ninth grade year in 1977. My friend, Kelly Morris, asked if I would be her escort in the homecoming court and I gladly did so. In the picture of Kelly and me is another couple, just behind us. Guess who? It was my good friend Robert Davidson and a girl named Alison Hardin. Alison and I had mutual friends but we didn't even really know each other. I don't think we even talked during our ninth grade year even though I was on the basketball team (starter) and she was a cheerleader. A year later three of my buddies and I were going to a concert and asked Kelly to go along with us and invite a friend. So she invited Alison Hardin.

I learned later that Alison didn't really want to go that night. She did so to please her mom who was worried because her daughter was experiencing some teenage doldrums. That night while waiting in line for the concert—for some reason—we started talking. There was a spark. I asked her out for the next weekend and she said yes. We went to see *The Champ* starring Jon Voight and little Ricky Schroeder. Really sad ending to that movie when the champ dies, but I held back my tears. That was real hard, I'll be honest. But, I was cool. Alison and I never dated anyone else again. Now here we are twenty-one years later with a house payment and three children of our own, living in the same town we grew up in.

Funny the twists and turns that make up a life.

Seemingly small decisions can often have profound implications. What would have happened had Alison told her mom she didn't want to go to the concert that evening? Who knows?

Marriage is a gift from God. He ordained it. His perfect will is that one man marry one woman and that they stay together for a lifetime. Sadly, only about 50 percent of American couples follow this plan. But we should celebrate when couples do stay together, ". . . for better or for worse, for richer and for poorer, in sickness and health, till death do us part." For Alison and me, we've some great examples to follow, which, quite frankly, I think is a key. Alison and I only have one living grandparent each. But between all four sets of grandparents—close to 250 years of marriage—there was not one divorce. In fact, Dad's parents were married sixty-seven years before Mama Wildmon died. And both sets of parents have both been together for over thirty-five years. Quite a family legacy we have.

One of the leading contributors to the social and moral problems that our country is experiencing is the break-up of the home. That's no secret. Maybe we are not doing enough as parents and as churches to model real commitment in front of our children and teenagers. Maybe too many ministers marry people they hardly know or have spent little time with in pre-marital counseling. Maybe we have become so intoxicated with the wine of self-gratification that it's hard to care about anything but ourselves, our wants, and our desires—however temporal and shortsighted they may be. I don't know all the causes for divorce, but I do know couples who marry today often take the casual attitude of, "If it doesn't work we'll just get a divorce."

Well, I didn't write this to depress you. I wrote it to say that we all need to honor and celebrate marriage. We need to help couples stay together and encourage them to work out problems that threaten their homes.

And I wrote this to say "Happy Anniversary!" to my bride of fifteen years. Now if we can do fifteen years three more times we will be within seven years of Mama and Papa Wildmon's family record. That would be really cool.

Two Things to Remember

1. "Marriage should be honored by all" (Hebrews 13:4 NIV).
2. I am really, really glad Alison obeyed her mom and came to the concert that night.

SNOW

As much as I love living in the Deep South, there is one serious disadvantage to residing in the land of cotton and it has nothing to do with the fact that old times here are not forgotten. No, the downside of life in the South is that we get very little snow. To some of my fellow Southerners this is a good thing. But for me, it's a bummer. There's nothing quite as beautiful as a blanket of pure white snow covering my backyard and the open field beyond. I absolutely love it. I get green with envy when I see my friends in Vermont, Minnesota, or Colorado getting a foot of snow at Christmastime.

But that's not the reason I write here. The reason I write is my utter frustration with a modern science known as meteorology. Heard of it? This, my friends, is the study of an object commonly known as the parking meter. An object you and I pass by most every day without paying it much attention. I'll tell you what, before we continue I think it would behoove us to look up the word "meteorology" in the dictionary. No, let's go one better and look up the word in the World Book Encyclopedia. Okay, here we go. We are walking down the hall and we are picking out the M encyclopedia off the bookshelf which, from the looks of it, has never been cracked even though I—in the name of being a responsible parent—paid $1,000 for this set of books three years ago. There are what, twenty-two volumes in this set? That comes to about $46 per book. Hey, wait a minute, have *any* of these been used? Ever? A random check tells me the answer to this question is NO, they have not. Unbelievable. That's it—no more computer games. We are going to have ourselves a little family conference tomorrow, I'll tell you that. When I was a kid we didn't have all these fancy computers to turn our brains into mush. No, we had good old-fashioned television do that for us. And like good American children we used World Book Encyclopedias regularly to copy verbatim whatever the World Book said about a given subject like "volcano" or "indigestion" and then turned it in to our teachers as our own report. High academic standards we had back then. Are those days gone forever? I certainly hope not. Arise, oh children of the seventies! We simply must bring back that great tradition of plagiarizing the World Book if there is to be any hope for America's young people.

I'll tell you what else is unbelievable. I have gotten us way off track in this story. My apologies.

Now where were we? Oh yes, we were looking up

the word "meteorology" in the World Book. Now we are opening up the book and we are flipping through the pages quickly but we come upon pictures of—what's this?—the state of Maine. Boy, aren't these pretty? I've always wanted to visit Maine in the fall and see— what's wrong? Move on and get to the point, you say. Well, now, aren't we a little edgy? Okay, keep flipping and here we have it, Meteorology. Starts with an M. Here's what it says: "Meteorology is the study of the earth's atmosphere and the variations in atmospheric conditions that produce weather."

Hmm? What kind of book is this? It doesn't say anything about parking meters. Nothing. Could this be one of those rare moments, like when the planets align, that I am somehow mistaken? Well, maybe so. What- ever the case, while we're on the subject of weather I might as well tell you what I think of it. Fact is, I like weather. Really. It gives us something to talk about when we're bored with one another. But one element about the weather I don't appreciate is when they—the weather people—tell me that there is a winter storm headed my way with three to five inches of snow expected and then it doesn't snow a lick. Happened last night. Again.

The possibility of a snowstorm makes my heart beat fast with excitement. So don't tell me, weather people, it is going to snow and then you, weather peo- ple, can't deliver on your promise. You've done this to me time and time again since I was a kid and, quite frankly, I'm tired of it and I'm not going to take it anymore. To philosophize on this, I will simply say to you weather people: Liar, liar, pants on fire.

Aside from the emotional distress that you weather people have caused me over the years with your false promises of "heavy snowfall expected," you people also did severe damage to my academic career which affected my Permanent Record. Many times—oh, yes, we remember them well—many times you people told me snow was definitely coming down from Memphis and going to fall on Lee County, thus closing down the Tupelo City Schools, which meant that I wouldn't have that science or math test. And so what do I do, being a tender child with a trusting heart? I spend all night, face pressed against the window, waiting for the flakes to begin falling, never bothering to do anything— which would be a total waste of time—like studying, for instance. "Why study?" I would call up Rusty Wilkinson and say. "The weatherman says we're gonna get so much snow. We'll be out of school for a week, man, no doubt."

Ten o'clock, no snow. Eleven o'clock, no snow. I'm getting sleepy now. Midnight. Snow? Nope. *Well, I've got to get some sleep,* I would say to myself. *I've got a big day of snow-filled fun tomorrow and I'm going to be rested and ready to go. Nice Mr. Weatherman wouldn't lie to a kid like me.*

Oh, did I have a lot to learn about life. Six A.M. Look outside and what do I see? Grass and asphalt, that's what. What dark, painful memories these are. Time and time again you weather people lied to this trusting little boy with a tender heart. And time and time again this trusting little boy with his tender heart failed his science and math tests. Why? Because weather people lie, that's why. They lie a lot. And without remorse.

Vent, Tim. Let it out. This is good for the soul.

Thank you, I believe I will.

I'm sorry, weather people. Please forgive my rants. (Note to you readers: This is a false apology much like the false forecasts weather people give all the time.) No seriously, I know you weather people are only going by your computer models and so you can't be held responsible for leading little children on. But I'll tell you what you can do for us if you really want to get back in our good graces. What you can do, for once, is come on TV and admit when you were wrong. That's right. No blaming the National Weather Service or computer models or anything like that. Just like the rest of us on our jobs, you must take full responsibility for your words and actions.

Let me give you an example of what I'm talking about. Let's just suppose—and I know this is strictly a hypothetical situation—but let's just suppose you told us out here in TV Land that it was going to snow five inches last night. And let's—for the sake of argument—suppose you were dead wrong and it didn't snow a lick. For once, here's what I would like you to say:

"Well, ladies and gentlemen, boys and girls, last night I stood right where I am standing now and told you, in no uncertain terms, that it was going to snow two inches overnight. Okay, so I told you it was going to snow five inches. And, as you can see for yourself if you look out your window, we didn't quite make it there. In fact, truth be told, I was five inches off the mark. I, my dear people, was wrong. I was terribly wrong. I said five inches of snow, you counted on five inches of snow, my own children were counting on five inches of snow, and, well, I failed you. I let down my *own* family! for goodness' sake. If my wife is watching, Honey, I want you to know that I'm sorry. I feel awful about the whole thing. In fact, Sweetheart, honestly, I never really wanted to be a weatherman in the first place. I'm tired of living a lie, Baby. It was just all that pressure your parents put on me to finish weather school, get my degree, and someday be a senior meteorologist on the Weather Channel so I could provide you with the Great American Dream your folks said you deserved. I'm sorry to break this to you here, Honey, on live television. But what is it I'm trying to say to the rest of you people? What I'm trying to say is. . .is. . .is, that tonight we have a 50 percent chance of snow with accumulations of two to four inches expected in the northern part of the state and one to three in the southern part. And you can take that to the bank. Dan, back to you."

Well, even with all of today's technology, we can

never really know for sure exactly what the weather is going to do. However, we can know the Creator of the weather. He is trustworthy. And He doesn't mislead trusting children with tender hearts. In fact, His heart is the softest of all.

One of the great attributes of God's character is that He is consistent. He is reliable. He is not one way today and then another way tomorrow. The Bible puts it this way in the Old Testament book of Malachi 3:6: "For I am the LORD, I do not change" (NKJV). And in the New Testament the same sentiment is expressed in Hebrews 13:8: "Jesus Christ is the same yesterday, today, and forever" (NKJV).

So we can see, that unlike the weather—or those who forecast it—the Lord God can be trusted to be faithful. He is our Rock.

Now, I've been wondering. Do we have to forgive weather people who miss the mark, thereby destroying the academic futures of children like me? And does it snow in heaven? This is one little kid who certainly hopes so.

TWO THINGS TO REMEMBER

1. God remains the same always. He is unchangeable.
2. You folks in the North could blow a little more snow down Dixie way. Only, don't send us more than three inches or we'll have to call out the National Guard.

GLORY DAYS

It was the first week of March, and Alison had picked me up from work with two of the Terrific Three. (I'm really into positive-speak right now, so I'd appreciate it if you would just let me call people and things what I want to without saying I'm out of touch with reality.) Walker, my four-year-old, was at a friend's house. Wriley and Wesley, ages ten and eight, were in the back taking turns with the Gameboy. There are times I love that little machine. And there are times I hate it. It's a blessing when you need a break and it occupies their time. It's a curse when you have to yell out the child's name four times when you're getting out of the van for Sunday school. And on that last high-pitched shout is when one of the other children opens the van door for all the other folks in the parking lot to hear, isn't it?

". . .turn that dead blame thing off, boy, before I crush it under the van wheel! Do you hear me or are you also deaf?

"Oh, good mornin', Mrs. Jones. Lord's blessed us with a beautiful day, hasn't He?"

It was cool this particular March afternoon and

somewhat windy. Alison had decided she wanted to stop and vacuum the van out. If cleanliness is next to godliness then the Lord is at this very time constructing Alison a beautiful mansion right next to St. Peter's. And the angels are cleaning as they build. No unused two-by-fours or paint buckets lying around unless they're stacked and put away neatly.

I was tired and just wanted to lay the passenger seat back and relax.

"Why is it always cold and windy when you want us to open every door in the van?" I said.

"Oh, it won't take but a couple of minutes; you'll survive," she responded.

That's what she says about everything I complain about.

So we pulled up, Alison opened the van doors, pulled the mats out, and began popping quarters in. I moaned and grunted as I looked out the side window. There was a fellow, looked about in his mid-fifties—walking around the car wash picking up paper and cans. Nice-looking guy. Clean-cut, as my mama used to say. *Hey, that guy looks familiar,* I said to myself. He glanced over my way and I smiled and waved. *Hmm, where do I know that face from?* I looked away, thought for a moment, and looked back at him. He had on a blue jacket and was wearing a green golfer's cap. *Hey, that looks a lot like Coach Barron, my basketball coach in high school. I think it is Coach Barron.* He looked back at me and it was one of those moments where you see someone, they see you, and you both know you've known each other from somewhere, sometime. I decided to make the first move.

"Hey, are you Coach Barron?" I yelled, getting out of the seat. He couldn't hear me clearly because my beloved had that machine wide open and was bouncing all over the van. She was in a state of bliss. Sick, isn't it?

"Excuse me?" he responded as he came over closer to where I was.

"You're Coach Barron, aren't you?"

"Yes, I am."

"You probably don't remember me, but I'm Tim Wildmon. I was one of your players on the B team at Tupelo High."

"Oh, yes, when exactly was that?"

"Well, let's see. It would have been 1978–79; it's been twenty years ago," I said. I couldn't believe I was saying "high school" and "twenty years ago" in back-to-back sentences. Had it been that long ago already? I glanced over to my reflection in the side window. Another chin, a lot less hair. Yes, it had been twenty years.

The years had been good to Theodus Barron. He had slimmed down, he looked healthy, and now had a few gray hairs peeking out from under his cap. We talked about our team; I introduced him to Wriley and Wesley and reminded him that he taught with Mom at Milam Junior High for several years.

"Oh yes, Mrs. Wildmon. Friendly lady. Taught. . ."

"Home economics."

"Right, home ec. How is she doing these days?"

The vacuum stopped long enough for Alison to come over and introduce herself.

"You've got great-looking children there, Tim and Alison," he said. "Better take care of them and be a good example."

I told him one of the reasons Mom stopped teaching was that, for her anyway, the kids had gradually become more and more of a control problem in class. He told me that, while he loved teaching and coaching, that was his experience as well. He stayed in the schools for twenty-nine years; Mom stayed about half that.

"It's a different world out there today," he said. "Kids today, they'll tell you real quick they don't care what you say. It used to be that when the kids misbehaved and got in trouble with the teachers or coaches they also got disciplined by their parents. Now the parents get a lawyer."

I shook my head in agreement as we both had a chuckle. He was kidding, but his humor wasn't far from reality. I hear they have metal detectors at Tupelo High School today. That seems to be the trend across the country. How sad. I read recently that over 50 percent of all violent crime committed against teenagers is done on campus or right around campus. Today, it's more dangerous on a typical high school campus than it is downtown late at night. Why? Simply because we have a moral meltdown in our beloved America. Families are falling apart and we parents are failing to instill what was once called "the fear of God" in our children. We fail to teach our kids right from wrong and then are surprised when they steal, lie, cheat, and act violently. We want to blame the teachers and administrators for not controlling the kids when we don't control them at home.

Well, we wound down our reminiscing of what was to me "the good ol' days" as I began to shiver and Alison's last quarters were—thankfully—used up.

"You know what, Tim, I'm not one to brag, but I never had a losing season in twenty-six years of coaching basketball," Coach Barron said and smiled.

"Hey, you were a good coach. You pushed us hard but you were always fair," I said.

"Well, you've got to go now and I've got to finish checking the place out here. I do this part-time to help a friend out. He owns this car wash. I tell you what, I'm feeling generous today. Why don't you pull your van up and I'll give you a free wash?"

"Really?"

"Sure, pull on up."

I pulled the car forward and sure enough, Coach began washing my van. It took him about ten minutes in the cool, early March air.

"He's such a nice man," Alison remarked, somewhat embarrassed that someone else was washing something that belonged to her.

As he finished, he tapped on the window. I rolled it down a little.

"Tell your mama I said hello."

"I sure will, Coach. I sure will."

As we drove out, Wriley parroted her mother. "He's a real nice man, Daddy."

Wesley—I could tell he was thinking.

"Dad?"

"Yeah, Wes."

"What's a B team?"

Two Things to Remember

1. We need to teach our children right from wrong—what used to be called "the fear of God." We also need to teach them to respect their elders and others in authority. These are timeless values.

2. As much as I liked and respected Coach Barron, still, by virtue of him keeping me on the bench for long stretches of time—like the whole game, like a lot of whole games—he really is responsible for my not having a chance at professional basketball. Oh, what might have been, had I not been relegated to picking pine splinters from my rear end.

TRANSFUSION AND TRANSFORMATION

One evening in January I was at home with the family when the phone rang. I rarely pick it up because it's rarely for me, and nine times out of ten it's someone wanting you to do something for them. Have you noticed this? Do your own survey at home and see if what I'm saying isn't true. When our phone rings it's usually for Alison or our ten-year-old daughter, Wriley. For some reason this has become the magic year for Wriley and phone calls. Thankfully, no boys are calling yet, but her giggly little girlfriends are letting their fingers do the walking a lot lately.

I must admit, I am amused at the things ten-year-old girls talk about. Teachers, clothes, toys, boys, homework, what she said about what he said, and, of course, other friends are the favorite topics. Imagine that. This is when females learn the fine art of gossip. My boys, Wesley and Walker, ages eight and four, and I stay away from all that gossip by doing something productive like watching football or basketball.

But this time when the phone rang, I picked it up.

"Is this Timothy Wildmon?" asked the voice on the other end.

This sent up red flags immediately because nobody calls me Timothy. I only use this name when I sign really important papers like at the bank or somewhere else. Times when I think my full name sounds better. The likelihood of someone named Timothy defaulting on a loan is much less than someone known as "Tim" is the way I see it. That's redneck logic, isn't it?

"Well, I go by Tim," I said.

"Mr. Wildmon, this is Donna from United Blood Services and we are experiencing a severe shortage of blood. It's so serious, some operations at the hospital are going to be postponed if we don't have some donors. We show that you gave last September and we were hoping you could come in and give again."

"Are you going to stick my finger again?"

"Well. . ."

"I'd rather have a double enema, Donna. I'll just be honest with you."

Donna was silent. I had caught her off guard with the double enema thing. I don't even know if there is such a procedure. She may have been wondering about it herself.

"I'm halfway kiddin', Donna. But I do hate the finger-sticking. But, sure, I'll be glad to come down there tomorrow."

"When can I schedule you for?"

"Oh, put me down for 2 A.M. Y'all are open after

the bars close, aren't you?"

"Actually. . . ."

"Donna, I'm kiddin' again. I'll stop."

"That's fine, Mr. Wildmon."

"I'll be there at two o'clock tomorrow afternoon."

The next day I ate a good lunch and headed on down to United Blood Services. I walked in, signed the register, and took a seat. Then I began reading a May 1979 edition of *Bassmasters*. Funny thing, bass looked exactly the same back then.

"Timothy Wildmon," the nurse said, looking to see which one of the three of us was me.

As I got up she escorted me back to the interview booth. This is where they check your blood pressure, stick your finger to draw blood, ostensibly to check your iron. I think they just do it for fun. Then she asked me all manner of bizarre and very personal questions.

"Did you travel to Angola between 1973 and 1975, and if so, did you use unclean needles to inject illegal drugs while drinking Diet Dr. Pepper and wearing a Tommy Hilfiger T-shirt, and how did that affect your intimacy with your significant other?"

"Can you repeat the part after the Diet Dr. Pepper? I was with you right up to that point."

"Were you wearing a Tommy Hilfiger T-shirt and how did that affect your intimacy with your significant other?"

"Well, that's a lot of question, ma'am. Where do you want me to start? It seems to me I was playing a whole lot of "kick the can" in 1973 and probably wouldn't have even had time to travel to Angola. Wore a St. Louis Cardinals T-shirt my mom bought me all summer. So, I am gonna say no to all the above."

Well, I made it through all that and went back down the hall to the room where they take your blood. I'm sorry. That's the room where you donate your blood. It took about twenty minutes, I guess. When it was all over, the nurse removed the syringe, put a Band-Aid on my arm and told me to drink plenty of liquids and not to skip a meal. Then I left, feeling pretty good about myself.

Maybe my donation saved somebody's life, I thought.

Driving back to the office I remembered all those personal questions the nurse had asked me. She wanted to find out what the chances were that I could have some sort of disease that would taint my blood. It didn't occur to me at the time, but I should have answered, "Yes, my blood is contaminated. You see, I was born with a serious disease. It's called sin and we all have it."

Then I thought about the One who came to Earth who had perfect blood—pure and undefiled. You see, Jesus Christ was the only Man who ever lived who was born without the disease of sin. And yet, Jesus gave His life—spilled His blood—for my sins. He gave His blood for Tim Wildmon. Why? So that I could have forgiveness of sin and fellowship with Almighty God. So that I could spend eternity with Him in heaven.

"Greater love has no one than this, that he lay down his life for his friends," Jesus said (John 15:13 NIV). Think about that; we are the Lord's friends. Oh, how precious the thought. Praise God in the highest!

Two Things to Remember

1. Jesus gave all for you and me. Read the Easter story today.
2. I still hate it when they prick my finger. Don't you? They say this is necessary but I'm just not so sure. They seem to enjoy it too much.

Q. What Role Did Julia Child Play in the Exodus of the Israelites from Egypt?

Barney Lamplighter of Boston, Massachusetts

A. Barney, first let me congratulate you on a great question. If you look through some of these other questions you will see why I think yours ranks right up there at the top. Why? Because it is a challenging question that gets my intellectual juices flowing. Now to your question.

Barney, since you brought up the name Julia Child, I am going to assume you know who she is. Now for others reading this, especially if you are under thirty, you probably need to ask someone older than you about Julia Child. Your parents are probably older than you, so ask them.

Julia Child is a world-renowned cook with her own television show on PBS. What is distinctive about Julia Child has nothing to do with the fact that she can probably make exquisite cuisine, rather, it is her extremely unusual voice. Let's just say her singing career was just a flash in the pan. Come to think of it, that may be where she got the idea to become a world-renowned cook. You know. Flash. Pan.

I am getting to your question, Barn, so stay with me. The information I just gave you is vital to answering your question.

Now, what role did Julia Child play in the Exodus of the Israelites from Egypt?

You remember, Barn, that Moses warned Pharaoh that if he didn't let God's people go, He, God, not Moses (although he was a great man), would send plagues and diseases that would give the Egyptians fits. God wasn't playing. He first sent the plague turning the river to blood which caused all the fish to die, the river to stink, and the Egyptians to discontinue using it as a source of drinking water.

Now if I'm Pharaoh, this would have been all I needed. I am convinced here. I would have arranged a first-class, red-carpet send-off for my new Israelite friends and basically given them anything they wanted. Maybe some new chariots to sweeten the deal—I would have even thrown in a couple of pyramids along the Nile River beach just in case they wanted to come back and vacation in the winter. But this "blood-in-the-river plague" did not sway Pharaoh one bit.

The second plague the Lord sent—and God can get real creative as evidenced by the first few chapters of Genesis—were billions and billions of frogs to cover Egypt. While this did bother and inconvenience

Egyptians, doubling and in some cases tripling commute time for many, the rednecks from southern Egypt actually were heard yelling, "Praise the Lord!" for this particular plague and many took a week's vacation just to go frog gigging with the family. "What a great bonding experience," many said. But this, even this plague didn't convince Pharaoh to let the Israelites go. (Again, like I said, the blood thing would have been enough for me.)

This is the point in history where Pharaoh developed a reputation for being really stubborn.

Anyway, we need to shorten this section, so let me just say that Pharaoh went on being stubborn and the Lord went on sending plagues which we will now list followed by a short bit of factual information about each.

1. *Lice*—A nightmare for the Cairo County School system.
2. *Flies*—Flyswatter stock went through the roof and the song, "Shoo fly, don't bother me," was first recorded by the Supremes.
3. *Disease on beasts*—Many "County Fair & Livestock Shows" reduced to just "County Fair."
4. *Boils on man and beasts*—Painful, but made for tasty shrimp and crawfish.
5. *Hail*—Not to be confused with "hell" which would have been the mother of all plagues.

6. *Locusts*—Again, the rednecks celebrated with the opening of locust season.
7. *Darkness*—Great for casino business along the Nile.
8. *Death for all the firstborn in Egypt*—No real commentary needed.

I can't stress enough here that if I had been Pharaoh, the river turning to blood (first plague) would have been enough for this hombre. (If you ever are a pharaoh, Barney, I hope you will learn this lesson from history and immediately let God's people go upon the first request.)

What is not mentioned in the biblical account, and we're not exactly sure why, is that the Lord sent one more plague on Egypt which absolutely broke Pharaoh's stubborn will. One night the Lord sent Moses and Aaron and a few friends of theirs out to set up large loudspeakers all around Pharaoh's compound. The Lord then instructed Moses to play that 1969 hit "King Tut" by Julia Child and Bob Dylan and, I quote but yet I paraphrase the Lord here, "Crank it up real loud!"

It worked. After twenty minutes Pharaoh—who could have doubled for Steve Martin—came out in his house robe and slippers and pleaded for Moses to stop. "OH, HEBREW PEOPLE, I BEG YOU, PLEASE, PLEASE, TURN THAT THING OFF, TAKE YOUR BELONGINGS, GO TO ANOTHER LAND, AND THROW THAT TAPE IN THE NILE ON YOUR WAY OUT! AND DON'T WORRY ABOUT

THE DEAD FROGS; WE'LL CLEAN UP! NO, LEAVE ME ALONE; I'VE GOT A BIG DAY AHEAD OF ME TOMORROW AND I ABSOLUTELY MUST GET SOME SLEEP!"

So, there, Barney Lamplighter, is the answer to your question. It just took a little explaining that most people aren't willing to listen to or explore for themselves. We must—together, Barney—fight this apathy among some people in this country who don't care anything about off-the-wall biblical history. Please do write again. I like your spunk.

Write On

I'm often reminded of our need to use the gifts and talents God gives us for His glory to advance His kingdom. Recently the Lord gave me a wonderful opportunity to do just this. I'll tell you about it in a moment.

I graduated from Mississippi State University in 1986. I really enjoyed the college experience except for one thing. Tests. I never could come around to liking exams. In fact, for about five years after I finished school I would have this recurring dream that I had a big test the next morning and I had forgotten to study for it. Sometimes I would wake up in the middle of the night and then have to remind myself that I had already completed school. Go dig my degree out of the closet. *There's no need to panic, Tim. Now go back to sleep,* I would tell myself.

I also had dreams that I went to school without any pants on. Just underwear. That one usually caused me to wake up in a cold sweat, thinking my life was over. I could never go out in public again. Although this

"Look! No pants!" dream isn't a topic I discuss often with others (there just never seems to be an appropriate time), I have had enough "late-night-just-before-you-go-to-sleep-men's-retreat" conversations to know I'm not the only one who's had this particular dream. Don't know why. Don't know what it means. My brother Mark is about finished with his doctorate degree in psychology. When he gets through, I'll ask for all of us and save the rest of you the embarrassment. Anyway, back to my waking up in the night "thinking I had a test" dream.

One of the reasons I experienced this phenomenon, I now believe, is that I wasn't big on preparation. I once waited until the last night to type a fifteen-page term paper that also had to be researched. Alison says there are times when she can still hear that old electric typewriter clicking in the night. (This was 1984, before personal computers became so popular.) Finished at 8:30 for a 9 A.M. class and made a B+. High risk, yes. But I was kind of proud of myself for seeing an academic challenge and meeting it head-on. But like most students, I enjoyed some subjects, so the learning part was easy. With others, I had to drag myself to class and force myself to listen. Oftentimes, Self would tell me he didn't want to listen and—to be quite honest—he didn't want to be there in the first place. Sometimes I won. Sometimes Self won. It was a constant battle.

After about a year of what I would call floundering

in business school, it dawned on me one day in the cafeteria. I was having breakfast by myself and reading the newspaper. This was my morning ritual. Now I enjoy good company as much as anyone, but give me a cup of coffee, a table off by itself, and a newspaper and I am one happy camper. Sports first, editorials second, and front page third. But it occurred to me one morning that I really enjoyed reading and writing (not big on arithmetic) and that maybe journalism was for me.

I visited a guidance counselor—one of twelve responsible for 14,000 students between the ages of eighteen and twenty-five. Not exactly the most stable of demographics.

"Mr. Guidance Counselor."

"Yes, student 1098694, how may I assist you?"

"You care about me don't you, Mr. Guidance Counselor?"

Phone rings.

"Paul, what's going on, buddy?" (Pause.) "Oh, no, you're not interrupting anything important."

Ten minutes later I make hand signals.

"Mr. Guidance Counselor, I really hate to break in here but. . ."

"Gotta run, Paul. I'll take the Cowboys and lay the five." (Hangs up phone.) "Yes now, Mister. . ."

"Wildmon, sir. 1098694."

"Right. Now spit it out, Mr. Wildmon. I've got several hundred students waiting to see me and you're just gonna have to work some of your problems out on your own. I'm not your mama here."

"I haven't told you any problems yet, Mr. Guidance Counselor."

"I'm sorry, Wilson, you're just going to have to reschedule and come back when you've got something substantive to talk about."

And so began my career change. I decided to study journalism. I wanted to be a writer. I began to really enjoy school. That was over fifteen years ago. Today, in my position as vice president of American Family Association, I am able to utilize this gift to defend and advance the Christian value system.

In addition to writing a monthly column in the *AFA Journal* and an occasional book like the one you are now reading, I also get some opportunities to write editorials and opinion pieces for other publications. *USA Today* recently called and asked me to write a response to their editorial promoting sex education. Their position called for more "sex education," i.e., condoms, et cetera—the usual "kids are going to do it so we might as well show them how to do it safely" liberal way of thinking. I wrote in defense of abstinence. I strongly emphasized the Christian view of sexuality. That piece was read by perhaps millions of people all over the country. Thank You, Lord. Thank You for the honor of using the gift You gave me to Your glory.

What I want to encourage you to do today is to think of the ways you can use the gifts and talents the Lord has given you. For instance, if you, too, are a writer, take the opportunity to write letters to the editor of your local newspaper. Did you know that these letters are the second most-read section of the paper behind the front page? People want to know what's on the minds of their neighbors—sometimes even more than they want to know what the paid columnist thinks about an issue. Well, the printed word can be very useful in communicating our message. I encourage you to look for ways, from the newspaper to the church newsletter, to write for our side.

Did you get all that? Well, I hope so. Because now I'm going to give you a test. This is not a dream. Okay, take out your paper.

Two Things to Remember

1. Use whatever gifts God has given you to serve Him and to serve His people. He expects no less from us.
2. As much as I enjoy the Internet, give me that old-fashioned newspaper. The kind that cracks and pops as you open it. There's something wrong with a "newspaper" a man can't get ink stains on his fingers from.

MOMMY DEAREST

Recently I was on a plane from Memphis to Dallas, en route to Phoenix, Arizona. The DFW International Airport is to jets what Mecca is to Muslims. They are drawn there. It is hallowed concrete. About midway through the one-hour flight I got into a conversation with the lady next to me. She was in her forties. I had overheard her say that she was in Tupelo the week before and that piqued my curiosity. Come to find out she was from the county just north of me—Prentiss County. She then introduced me to her mom who was sitting by the window. Nice lady, in her sixties. She told me they were from the small (and I'm talking Mississippi small, not New York small) New Site community and that sparked this comment from me.

"Oh, really? My mama went to high school at New Site in the mid-1950s. Played basketball. Once scored fifty-two points in a game," I bragged. I love telling this.

"Is that right?" the older lady said. "Well, guess what? My husband, who is sitting right behind us here, was the basketball coach during that time. What was your mama's name?"

"She would have been Lynda Lou Bennett. Parents were Bill and Eloise Bennett from up around Moore's Mill."

"Oh yes, I remember that young Bennett girl. She was a fine little player for Jack (Arnold)."

What? I remember thinking. *Ma'am, if scoring fifty-two points in a game doesn't make you more than a "fine little player," then I don't know what does. You need to upgrade your memory here. My mama was an excellent, dominating player who probably made your husband look like a much better coach than he actually was.* But, I didn't say it. It would have embarrassed Mama and she wasn't even there.

We talked some more and as we were gathering our stuff together to deboard the plane Mrs. Arnold introduced me to her Mr. Arnold.

"Jack, you remember that little Bennett girl that played for you back in the fifties?"

"Well, let's see. Yeah, I do remember Lynda."

"Well, this is her son. What did you say your name was again?"

"Bond. James Bond."

"What?"

(Note to readers here: Always take every opportunity to mess with people when you can. When someone has to stop and think about what you just said, it gives you the upper hand, allowing you to take the conversation whichever direction you wish. You can make a lot of money selling people things they don't need this way, if you are smart.)

"Tim Wildmon, ma'am," I said as I reached out to shake her husband's hand.

"Last I heard, your mom was living in Tupelo."

"Still is."

"I remember Lynda was a good player, worked hard, came from a good family. Did everything I asked her to do and more. But I had so many players it's hard to remember them all."

We continued for a few more minutes and then we bade adieu. Mama has always done everything life's asked of her and more. Most mamas have.

Each May Americans celebrate Mother's Day. The day, perhaps above all others, evokes emotion and memories for us. Granted, the memories are not positive for everyone. But for most folks reading this, you had a mama who tried to do her best for you. That's just the nature of moms. God made them that way. Even if your natural mom gave you up for adoption, I'll bet when she did so, she had the best of intentions at heart. As I said, God made mamas with a natural desire to nurture and care for their children. That in itself deserves celebration.

"The hand that rocks the cradle, rules the world," is the old saying.

My memories are of hot breakfasts on cold winter mornings. Mom believed that if we didn't have a good breakfast in our tummies, we wouldn't be able to do as well in school. If we didn't make good grades, it wouldn't be because the eggs weren't scrambled and orange juice wasn't served.

Mom had four children separated by eight years. Still, she would take us to swimming lessons, baseball practice, ballet, Girl Scouts, Boy Scouts, PTO, and whatever church activities we might have. Dad was the pastor. "If the pastor's kids didn't participate, it would be a bad example for the rest of the church" was Mom's way of thinking. Also, she took time to teach her children right from wrong. Burned it into us.

She didn't believe in harsh words, either. Wouldn't even let me call someone a "liar." Instead, she would tell me the person may have been "dishonest," or perhaps the accused was a "storyteller."

She also cooked great suppers, let us have a dog, tucked us in at night, took us see to Dr. Dale when we got sick, and taught cake decorating lessons at our church at night on a few occasions so she could buy something a little special.

Mom still makes the best pound cake in the world. And now she loves and cares for her five grandchildren who all live in and around Tupelo.

Like millions of ladies, perhaps your mom, she needs to be honored and shown appreciation often. Not just on the second Sunday in May.

There are a lot of problems in this world. Many of those problems are caused by people who have little regard for the traditional moral values that have served our country well for so long. We need more moms—and dads—to take raising their children seriously today. And the need to teach our kids the difference between right and wrong has never been greater. Indeed, the hands that rock the cradle, change the diaper, bandage the cut, straighten the tassel, encourage the mind, comfort the heart, and mold the character can make all the difference in the world.

And yes, you read that right. Sixty-two points in one game. I'm telling the truth. My mama didn't raise a storyteller.

Two Things to Remember

1. Exodus 20:12 reads, "Honor your father and your mother, that your days may be long upon the land which the LORD your God is giving you" (NKJV).
2. Seventy-two points. That's my story and I'm sticking to it.

MY WAY OR HIS WAY

With the possible exception of Elvis Presley, no other entertainer captured the hearts of Americans during the twentieth century more than Frank Sinatra did. I was vacationing with the family on Hilton Head Island when CNN reported the news of Sinatra's death. Although being a child of the seventies I could only name a couple of his tunes—"New York, New York" and "I Did It My Way" come to mind—it was still kind of sad seeing an American icon pass away. The Italian boy from Hoboken, New Jersey made it big. He could sing, no doubt about that. Frankly, if you'll excuse the pun, I had no idea Frank Sinatra had accomplished so much in his eighty-three years. Albums, movies—this man lived what a lot of people call the ultimate American dream. Fame. Fortune. Millions of records sold. Everybody loved Frank Sinatra.

A few days after his death, the funeral was a major news story. The television cameras captured a Who's Who from Hollywood, Washington, and New York, paying their last respects to their friend, the man they called "The Chairman of the Board." The day after his burial I was reading about the service. It seems Mr. Sinatra's daughter decided to put three items in his coffin as he was laid to rest in the southern California soil, things she thought the great entertainer would want to take with him if he could. The items were: A bottle of Jack Daniels, a pack of Camel cigarettes, and ten dimes. That was it. Some whiskey, a smoke, and some change to call home. I had to read the paragraph twice.

Later that night I was telling Alison about this. She looked at me with surprise and said, "What?"

"That's what they said," I responded.

"How sad. You would think they would have put something more important and more meaningful in his coffin."

"Well, yeah, I guess. But then, from what I've read, those things kind of symbolized his lifestyle. Drinking, partying, hanging out with the guys. That was his public persona. But you're right, kind of depressing, isn't it?"

"If that's what your family remembers you for, that's real depressing."

That made me think about what I would like placed in my coffin if I should ever die. (According to medical experts I've talked to, there is a 70 percent chance this could happen at some point in my life. That statistic has a 30 percent margin of error, according to these same medical experts.)

How about my Bible? Yes, the Scriptures are very important to me. But the truth is I need to read and cherish the Bible more.

How about a picture of my family? I love my wife and three children dearly. And I am a pretty good father, if I do say so myself. I think Alison and the kids would agree. So, to put a photograph of my family in with me would be true to what was important in my life.

Now what else? Perhaps this personal computer I am now writing on since I spend so much time in front of it. But if you included the screen, keyboard, speakers, *and* the printer, you're talking about a much bigger (and more expensive) coffin than I need or am willing to pay for with my life/death insurance monies that I would want Alison and the kids to have. Besides, it would probably be real hard to close.

What about an American flag? I love this country very much. In my mind, America, even with all her faults, is still the greatest country in the world.

You know, the truth of the matter is, we can't take anything with us when we pass from this world to the next. Anything material, anyway. The Egyptian pharaohs tried to take everything with them. That's why we have great pyramids. But you know what? While I appreciate the hard work and building skill of the ancient Egyptians as much as anyone, really, all that work was for nothing. And building pyramids, my friends, with your hands and back was a lot of hard work. In fact, I'll bet there were times when some of the average blue-collar Egyptians wanted to tell Mr. Pharaoh what he could do with his pyramid ideas. *Give me a bass boat and the Nile,* many must have thought.

Archeologists have dug into these tombs and discovered the pharaohs' possessions still there. Perhaps you've been to one of the traveling exhibitions of these artifacts and seen them for yourself. Although very powerful men, even the pharaohs could not take their riches and treasures with them.

Later in the conversation with Alison, I made an observation. It was something I said without too much thought. Just one of those "driving-down-the-road-you-can-say-anything-to-your-wife-and-she'll-accept-you" kind of comments. Said I, "You know, when you boil life down, what really matters is; do you believe in Jesus and do you care for others? That seems to be the bottom line to me."

Alison agreed. (Smart woman, Alison.)

I know that there are a lot of variables and many additional concerns and passions in life for most of us. There's nothing wrong with that. However, in the final analysis, that about sums up our purpose in life. Jesus was asked in Matthew 22:36: "Teacher, which is the greatest commandment in the Law?" Then, "Jesus replied, 'Love the Lord your God with all your heart and with all your soul and with all your mind.' This is the first and greatest commandment. And the second is like it: 'Love your neighbor as yourself.' All the Law and the Prophets hang on these two commandments" (Matthew 22:37–40 NIV).

"You can't take it with you when you die" is a wise and truthful saying. Isn't that good? Well, you can thank me for it. I made it up one day while I was driving down the road just letting great thoughts roll off my tongue as Alison balanced our checkbook and listened.

She then remarked, "Well, from the looks of this checkbook, that's not going to be a problem."

Smart woman, that Alison.

Two Things to Remember

1. Philippians 2:3 says, "Let nothing be done through selfish ambition or conceit, but in lowliness of mind let each esteem others better than himself" (NKJV).
2. Smart woman, that Alison. Married me, didn't she? What more proof do you need?

Like You See 'Em

There are few things more distinctively American than Little League baseball. Yes, they play baseball other places in the world but not like we do here.

White lines on brown dirt. The smell of freshly cut grass. All the boys in colorful uniforms, wanting to make their daddies proud. Grown men—coaches—who look funny, having traded in their work clothes for larger versions of the same uniforms the boys wear. Mamas who keep popping up from their lounge chairs between conversations about how busy their summers are in order to cheer on their sons or yell some encouraging words to an umpire. (More on this in a moment.)

Soft drinks, hot dogs, the aroma of burgers on a grill. . . Dodging foul balls and praying one doesn't hit your windshield. . . Players shouting "Hey batter! Batter!" to the other team's batter in hopes of breaking his concentration. . . (They don't do this in the major leagues by the way, only in the Little League.) All the above help make up Little League baseball, American style. And, of course, there are the fathers who are reliving their younger days on the diamond through their sons. Some men take this too far. I've promised myself I wouldn't. But still, every dad wants his son to do well if he plays sports. We're just made that way. When they get a hit, our hearts race. When they strike out, we are pained.

Another common occurrence in Little League baseball is that—most of the time—it is the parents who must bring everything together for the game to take place. It's usually a parent who chalks the lines and cuts the grass. If it rains, it's usually a parent who spends an hour or two getting the field in playing condition. Parents always keep the score books. Our league can only afford one umpire who works the plate, so the field umpire is usually—you guessed it—a parent.

Well, I had managed to avoid this job for most of our season. Jeff Hardin, Jacob's dad, had been willing and able most of the time. Then, one evening near the season's end, Jeff was unavailable for duty and so Gerald (pronounced "Jurl" in the Deep South, don't ask me why) Powell—one of our coaches—hollered out to me from the dugout.

"Tim, can you umpire the field?" He gave me that "we really need you, man" look.

"Well, yeah, I guess so," was my response from the lounge chair gallery behind home plate.

So I trotted out between first and second base as the home plate umpire yelled out, "Batter up!"

This feels kind of weird, I thought to myself. *I haven't done any umpiring in years and I certainly am not impartial here. I want Wesley's team to win.* Wesley was playing center field. *Oh well,* I said to myself, *just remember the umpire's credo and call 'em like you see 'em and you'll do fine.*

Well, we rocked along there for about three innings. The hardest part was not giving Wesley vocal encouragement when he was batting. The words were in my chest and throat wanting desperately to come out. But I restrained myself, thus holding high the dignity of the umpiring profession.

In the fourth inning one of the opposing team's players hit a ball into center field. Wesley ran up, camped under the ball, and then began to lose it in the lights. I could see what was about to happen if he didn't get his glove in front of his face and sure enough it did. The ball came out of the thick night air and, with gravity's full force, slammed into the right side of my son's face. I had to make the call at second before I could suspend the action to go check on Wesley. I rushed over. His mouth was bleeding some and his lip was swelling up, but there were no broken bones or eye damage, thank the Lord. All of the coaches were out with me checking on Wesley and some of the players were asking if he was all right. He had grimaced and cried just a little but we were about ready to break up the scene and get back to baseball when *she* broke through the small gathering. My wife. Wesley's mama had made her way out to center field.

"Are you okay, baby?" She bent down and looked him in the eye. "You probably need to come out."

"No he doesn't," I injected. "They don't have any other players and the team can't be without a center fielder. He'll be okay. It's just a little bleeding and a swollen lip. He can play."

"Do you want to stay in?" Alison asked Wesley, letting him be the final decision maker. He shook his head "yes," he wanted to continue. So Wesley's mama left the playing field and I went back to my station. I kept looking out at Wes to make sure he was okay while I was gaining more confidence in my role as umpire.

My calls were getting louder. Instead of "He's out!" I was saying "He's OUT!" Instead of barely making hand gestures, I began to use my whole body to indicate my call. There was one hit down the line in right field and I had to run out and see if it was fair or foul. When it hit the chalk I threw my arms back toward the field signifying a fair ball. Pulled a muscle in my side. I tried not to cry, but it hurt. But I looked like a Big League ump out there. I was in control. And I was becoming a control freak.

Then with two outs in the last inning—and our team at bat and my son Wesley on second base—I made a call that would become my signature call as an umpire. When someone, one day, records the history of the Saltillo, Mississippi, Youth Baseball Association, it is the following call that I will be remembered for. Not for all the other things I did, such as rounding up foul balls, taking my four-year-old to the restroom, going back to the car for another chair, no. It is this play. I'll describe it for you.

There I was, positioned on the edge of the outfield grass between first and second. I've already told you that, haven't I? Anyway, the pitcher fires home and the ball gets away from the catcher. This happens every other play in Little League. Wesley, seeing what has happened and following the lead of his coach, darts toward third base with great speed and determination, just like his old man of yesteryear. The catcher retrieves the ball quickly and fires down to third base. (If you would like to add more drama here, please imagine this scene in slow motion with the theme from *Chariots of Fire* playing in the background.) As the ball arrives into the third baseman's glove, he turns to tag Wesley who is leaning away from the third baseman while trying to get his foot in under him and to the bag before he is tagged. Kind of a half slide. It was a bang-bang play. From where I stood, though, he was out.

"He's out!" I said loudly. I was oblivious to the fact that the home plate umpire had given the safe sign, but I was much more forceful than he by this time.

Coach Powell, coaching third, looked across the field at me and asked for clarification, "What does the umpire say?"

"The runner on third is out!"

"All right then, that's it. The game's over."

Immediately I sensed a certain level of hostility from "our" dugout. I heard voices saying, "Wesley was safe. Can you believe that call?" and the like. "Yeah, Wesley's own dad called him out and he was easily safe. What a way to end the game."

As I walked toward "our" dugout I got none of Wesley's teammates' usual responses to my "good game, guys" comments. Clearly, I was not a friend of the team any longer.

I went over to the other umpire hoping for reinforcement for my call.

"From where I was, he was out," I said. "What did you think?"

"Well, it was close. I thought he was safe. But it was close."

Oh great, I thought. I walked through the gate and started toward our team's cheering section. These usually friendly faces looked back at me without expression. Some shook their heads. Some looked away. Still others mumbled under their breath. Then I heard someone say, "I'm gonna have to have a word with that umpire." The voice was that of my bride of fourteen years. But tonight, she was more Wesley's mom and less my bride.

"What kind of call was that?" She looked at me in a way that told me she had already answered the question for herself.

"What do you mean? From where I stood, he was

out. Barely, but the tag beat his foot to the base."

"Uh, huh. Funny, the home plate umpire, who clearly had a better angle, called him *safe*."

"Really? I didn't even notice. A good umpire calls the plays as he sees them, baby."

"Your son gets his face smashed in with a ball and then you call him *out* at the end the game when he was safe. I hope you can sleep with yourself tonight."

Alison didn't shout at me, thankfully, but she was half serious and half wanting to give me a hard time for calling her baby "out."

One of the hardest things in life is trying to be objective about ourselves and our family. Because of our emotions, it's difficult. We all know people who are always making excuses for themselves or for their children. When their children don't make good grades, they first blame the teacher. When they don't make the play, they blame the coach or another player. When their children get in trouble, they blame other kids for being a bad influence on their children. Oftentimes the children grow up unable or unwilling to take responsibility for their actions because they've been trained to find fault with others instead.

Now I am not talking about families sticking together. I'm glad blood is thicker than water. I don't know where that saying came from, but defending the ones we love is only natural and often serves a positive purpose. But not at the expense of truth. To deny reality—or truth—in the name of shielding ourselves or loved ones from criticism or responsibility that is justly deserved, at the end of the day, only hurts the one we are trying to help.

I have to tell you, I was proud of Wesley that night. I asked him if he was safe. He told me he thought so, but Coach Powell told the team to respect the umpire and accept the call without complaint. Come to think of it, I was proud of Coach Powell that night too. Glad to have my son playing for a coach who would encourage personal responsibility and respect for authority.

Now as for Wesley's mom, well, let's just say it took her a day or two to see the light. And as for me, I'm not one to complain, but I sure hope I don't ever have to make that kind of call again. Sleeping on my backyard grass gives me a rash. Calling 'em like you see 'em does have its downside.

Two Things to Remember

1. In life it is wise to strive to be objective and honest with ourselves. This is most difficult to do. Especially when it comes to our own lives. Start a relationship with someone you trust to be transparent with you and hold you accountable for your daily walk with the Lord.
2. Can I go back and change that call? It sure would make the rest of my life a whole lot easier.

TITANIC PROBLEM

In 1987 my dad decided to buy a boat. I don't exactly remember what prompted this decision, but boating is something the whole family could enjoy—even those who don't like to ski—and so I think that's the reason he had the idea. Not wanting to go all out for a new boat, because, basically a new boat cost a whole lot of money (which Dad said he didn't have after sending his four children through college), Dad began to watch the want ads for used boats.

One Saturday morning there appeared an advertisement for a 1977 Glastron ski boat in "excellent condition." The owner lived about fifty miles from Tupelo so Dad, my brother Mark (eight years my junior), and I drove down that morning to take a look at this boat said to be in "excellent condition." The gentleman, a farmer, said his two sons had used the boat when they lived at home, but they had grown up and moved away. The boat had been sitting under a shed for a few years but looked like it had been well taken care of. So the fellow gave Dad a really good price and we bought it.

Well "we" didn't actually buy it. Dad did. Mark and I were men of little means, which is a nice way of saying we were poor folk with little or no bargaining power. Well, "little" is a reach. Truth is, Mark and I had "no" bargaining power. But we were hard workers. Sometimes. When we were skiing anyway. And we had love.

The following Saturday we took this fine "new" boat out on the Tennessee-Tombigbee Waterway to show her off, let loose that Mercury 150, and blow past any ski boats, sailboats, or paddleboats that dared to challenge us. Also, I was looking forward to a boat that could actually pull me straight up out of the water unlike my friend's small fishing boat, which we had once tried to rig up into what amounted to a redneck surprise. You've seen people like us out on the lake. We're the ones you laugh at. No, my buddies and I, we didn't have much money. But we had fun and we had a boat with rope. Pitiful little motor, though. Which is one of the reasons you laugh at people like us out on the lake. One day, perhaps on your deathbed, you'll look at the times you pointed at, mocked, and jeered at people like my buddies and me. Poor people who couldn't afford a real ski boat with a real motor. And you'll regret making fun of us. I hope you feel real guilty too.

But this boat of ours was nice. Despite the fact that it was ten years old, it was in good condition—as far as the looks go anyway.

Well, we got out into the middle of the waterway.

Dad was driving, and Alison, Mark, and I were waiting for a good place to ski or ride the inner tube. Man, this baby was humming. Cutting across the water looking good. Once we found a good spot, we stopped, Mark jumped onto the tube, and we put some rope between him and the boat. We were excited. Here we were on the waterway with our own ski boat. Feeling kind of proud and puffy, I have to be honest with you. Dad pulled the rope tight and Mark gave him the big thumbs-up.

"Let's do it!" yelled Mark with a big grin and a thumbs-up.

"Hit it!" I relayed to Dad.

Dad pushed the throttle forward. We were starting to move. Ten, fifteen, now twenty miles an hour. We continued to gain speed, we were all smiles, when all of a sudden there came a loud cracking sound from the rear of our fine new ski boat that was in "excellent condition." Dad pulled back the throttle as Alison went to see what had caused the noise. As I pulled up the little skirt that separated the gas tanks from the passengers I immediately recognized two major problems:

A. The wooden back panel of the boat was cracking open. And. . .

B. Huge amounts of water were gushing into our ski boat, which was in "excellent condition."

It was clear that if this continued for a couple more minutes our "fine new" ski boat in "excellent condition" would be at the bottom of the Tennessee-Tombigbee Waterway.

"Get to shore or we're gonna sink!" I yelled to Dad, who himself saw the huge cracks in the rear hull.

All the while Mark was looking at us unable to hear what all the commotion was about because the Mercury 150 was still running.

"Untie Mark! We don't have time to pull him in," Alison told me. So all Mark could see was me taking his rope off the boat, throwing it off into the water, and then us speeding away. You should have seen the perplexed, dumbfounded look on his face. As we moved swiftly away I tried to yell something at him but I knew he couldn't understand a word I said. He jumped up on his knees and threw his hands into the air. We were leaving my baby brother out in the middle of the waterway all alone looking like a drunk who didn't realize he had drifted out to sea.

We raced to the shoreline and were able to pull the boat up out of the water before it sank. As long as we were moving fast it wasn't taking on water.

Our new ski boat looked great to the casual eye. It was sleek and smooth. The motor purred. But on the inside it was rotten. So rotten that when the first real test of strength came along it ripped apart from the inside out.

I thought about that boat the other day. I thought

about how America is a lot like it. In many ways, we are tearing away at our country's moral fabric calling right "wrong" and wrong "right." We say the economy is good, so what's the importance of values and character?

Yes, when you look at America, the economy is doing very well. We are the most affluent and most educated people in the history of the world. Who among us can't get a meal? And yet, we have lost our moral compass. We no longer know right from wrong or—perhaps worse—we no longer care. Money has become our god. We need to turn to the Lord—who is our bulwark, as Martin Luther wrote in that great hymn in 1529—and repair the widening cracks on our boat before we take on too much water and it's too late. Like the Titanic, we've been hit by an iceberg and yet maintain a false sense of pride and arrogance as if we are the unsinkable ship. Well, we're not, my friends. God doesn't care about America's money and might. He cares about our national character.

About Mark, well, he was a mere speck on the horizon when we finally got out of the water. When we got back from lunch he was barely recognizable, but moving toward the shore. When we got back from supper and pulled him out of the water his eyes were rolled back in his head and he was mumbling unintelligible things that sounded like "never forgive" and something about "dodging barges."

Two Things to Remember

1. Things aren't always what they seem to be. We need to check our lives from the inside out and let the Lord shine His light on our hearts, our motives, and our desires.
2. If I ever buy a boat myself, I think I'll name it "Redneck Surprise" just for ol' times' sake.

AFTERTHOUGHTS

Here we are again. The end of another venture into literary excellence. Have you been moved? Have you been inspired? Have you been challenged? Have you been dozing? Just what have you come away with as a result of reading *My Life as a Half-Baked Christian?* I want to know. If you will, take out a clean sheet of paper and write down for me ten things that have made you a better person as a result of reading this book. Now I want you to use complete sentences, avoid dangling participles, and whatever you do, please, no split infinitives. Say you don't know what a split infinitive is? Well, neither do I, but I'm told I use way too many of them. In fact, I may have just used two in a row and didn't even know it.

I don't know about you, but for me, God's lessons are often taught in the everyday things of life. I guess that is why I enjoy writing about everyday things. Okay, so I occasionally write about some crazy everyday things of life. Many authors sell a lot of books writing about living from miracle to miracle. Many,

many authors write about the Last Days. A lot of authors write about how to lose weight. And then there are writers like me. Maybe I should change topics and sell more books. You know, now that I'm thinking about it, maybe I could put together a book combining all three of these hot-selling topics. How about "How to Miraculously Lose Weight While You Go Through the Last Days" by Tim Wildmon. Oh, this is it, my friends. I have struck gold! What I could do then is have five or six sequels and become an incredibly wealthy individual. Yes, I could be a rich man and buy a big boat and a villa on the beach! But, rest assured, I would still mingle with you, the little people, from time to time. How about these titles. . .

- How to Keep Losing Weight After You've Waited on the Last Days for a Long Time
- Miracles Happen to Those Who Avoid Ice Cream During the Last Days
- The Last Days Are Here Again for Those Who Have Miracles Handy and Eat Right
- It's a Miracle! How to Lose Inches Off That Waistline by Reading about the Last Days
- Miracles and Healthy Diets for Those Who Haven't Had a Last Day Today

What about it? Am I a publisher's dream come true

or what? Now, I trust you will not attempt to steal my ideas here.

Seriously, thanks for taking time to join me here inside these covers. I suppose if you've read this far, you are a little bent like me. We see life's glass half full. Finding humor along life's winding road of bumps and potholes makes our journey a whole lot more enjoyable.

Let me encourage you to keep holding on to the promises of the Bible. After the laughter, after the tears, after the pain, after the rewards, after the split infinitives, after the joys and disappointments—at the end of the day—there is the promise of Jesus that He is with us through it all. He said He came that we might have life and have it more abundantly. If you don't know what that means, please take a little time to read the Gospel of John. It will change your life. And you will understand it is Christ who gives joy for today and hope for tomorrow.

Take care, my friend, and God bless until we visit again.

ABOUT THE AUTHOR

Tim Wildmon was born—if you care—in Houston, Missouri, in March of 1963. He was small as a child. Even smaller as an infant. He later moved to Atlanta, Georgia, when he was one year old. There he tried to get work as a sports anchor for CNN to help out the family as his dad was attending seminary at Emory University. CNN turned him down, however, citing a lack of "camera presence" and told him "to come back in twenty years when you can walk and we actually have a network."

Tim grew up in Tupelo, Mississippi, and did a whole lot of things—both good and not so good—between kindergarten and his graduation from Mississippi State University in 1987.

Today he is vice president of the American Family Association, based in Tupelo. AFA is a national Christian ministry founded in 1977 to deal with moral issues and public policy. Tim also co-hosts a weekday radio talk program, "Today's Issues," heard on the 180-station American Family Radio network.

He speaks often to groups across the country, has

written editorials for *USA Today*, and has appeared on CNN (finally!). His hobbies include fishing, writing, and saying "we'll see" to his children. Tim and his wife, Alison, have a daughter and two sons.

To contact Tim:
E-mail twildmon@afa.net
Or write P.O. Drawer 2440, Tupelo, MS 38803.